PROUD HORSES
PROUD RIDERS

A Napoleonic war illustration, by an unknown French officer, showing three Cossack horsemen. Mounted on the small but sturdy horses of their people, they wear typical Cossack outfits, and still carry the traditional lance and knout, though they are also armed with rifles.

PROUD HORSES
PROUD RIDERS

Edited by Jean-Louis Nou
Assisted by Bertrand de Perthuis
with contributions from Jeannine Auboyer
Jean-François Ballereau, Michel Cartier, Kurumi Sugita

TABARD
PRESS

Tabard Press
27 West 20th Street
New York N.Y. 10011

ISBN 0-914427-21-0

Printed and bound in Spain

CONTENTS

PREFACE

'. . . I am the inhabitant of the steppe, I possess nothing, neither rare nor precious objects; Horses are my wealth . . .'

Let us imagine one of our distant ancestors deep in the forest, or peering from his cave . . . He sees an animal, a zebra or an ass . . . perhaps even a wild horse. A gust of wind catches a dried leaf which, whilst dancing in the wind, comes to rest on the neck of the animal. A squirrel jumps from a branch onto the neck of a wild ass. Perhaps our ancestor has a fancy to play leap-frog, and finds himself, by chance, sitting astride the animal. The horse, startled, then breaks into a gallop . . . . We can guess the rest: the history of man and horse may have had such a beginning.

At that time, the horse, if we are to believe the cave paintings in Altamira, Lascaux and South Africa, was still a wild animal. What is more, it was very likely a more difficult animal to hunt than the bulky wild ox or the sedentary bison, and its swiftness and vigilance were a more efficient means of defense than those of other species; and so, the capture of a horse being uncommon, it became a token of glory for the hunter. And rightly so; is not one of the finest examples of human intelligence man's ability to tame and skillfully exploit the special characteristics of this remarkable animal?

Proud Horses, Proud Riders examines a myth: that of the solitary rider who has existed throughout time, above all in legend, but sometimes in reality, and who still exists today in some parts of our earth. In such places people live with passion, if without learning; for us this is a dream: the horse rediscovered.

In this book the reader will find no details of riding techniques, schools, breeding or dressage . . . . I wanted to let imagination amble along towards an encounter with the horses of today as well as with those that history has engraved in stone and those that man has forged in metal or stylized in miniatures. The horse exists oblivious of frontiers, at all latitudes, with traits common to all, undivided. The horse is one of the most powerful of animals. It unites people in the most diverse of activities: travel, business, war . . . even prestige.

Once having rediscovered the horse of yesterday in archaeological evidence, we will return to the present by visiting the high places where the riders of today live, from the high plateaux of Upper Asia to the Arabian desert, from the blue mountains of the Maghrib to the plains of Argentina. Cavalcades in time, cavalcades in space: the king's horse, the horse of ritual and death, conquering riders, horse breeders, cattle drivers, or cowboys of the last century . . . .

Mongolia is a word, at the same time barbarous and familiar. It evokes epic conquests of Genghis Khan or Kubla Khan, nomads and conquerors, unifiers of a domain from China to Jerusalem, as well as patrons of the arts. Of course, the Mongols of today live differently, but the steppe remains eternal, and to see the silhouette of a lone rider appear on the horizon, seemingly from nowhere, riding towards a yurt which the eye can just make out, is a rare spectacle. It is, therefore, with these riders of the steppe, the sons of Genghis Khan, that the book will open. After all, does not the Mongolian coat of arms figure a lancer galloping at full speed towards the rising sun?

Following the steps of Marco Polo, we will return to China. In the kingdom of the great rivers, the horse no longer lives, other than in legendary tales of the burning earth, in horses of jade buried beside emperors and in horses of earth that archaeologists extract piece by piece from the soil. On to Japan, where it is in the traditional martial arts that we will meet with the horse. Next, we will travel across the Ganges in order to meet the horse of Vedic sacrifice: the mount of the Gods, a temple ornament, and a companion to Buddha. In the fascinating land of India, horses of yesterday and riders of today find themselves intimately mingled: traders' horses, riders of the Deccan plains, refined horses of royal families and mounts of maharajahs.

Leaving Persia, on the horse of Alexander, we will gallop across Mongol country to rejoin the charger of the Prophet, and discover that Arab horse who still haunts the lost cities of the Nabateens. The companions of the Prophet will lead us to the shores of the Atlantic. Then, in the high Djebels we will discover that the tradition of the Numidian riders of Carthage and the mounts of Sidi Okba are still alive and well.

In following the thread of history, we will visit the Umaiyad's Empire in Andalusia which marks its Arab imprint on the Andalusian horses. Meandering through Rocio is enough to prove that rider's outlook which is unique to the people of Seville; and in the south of France and Central Europe we will see that the prehistoric horse of Niaux or Lascaux still lives.

Horses of conquest . . . As we know, the course of history changed when Christopher Columbus set foot in the West Indies and when Cortez endeavored to seize the Aztec empire. Those faced for the first time with the Andalusian horse found out — a little late, alas! — that these strange animal creatures are a little less than gods. It is from this invasion of the conquistadors that through the centuries has come the image of the 19th century American West: Cowboys, Indians, the Pony Express and the rodeo.

Riders of the New World . . . In 1530 a German introduced the first horse into Venezuela. One hundred years later, all South America was converted: gauchos of the Pampas, Mexicans and Cangaceiros.

This voyage of rediscovery will take us to faraway places, into Indonesia, then into Australia, and finally to the cowboys of the New World, who maintain the tradition of the Mongolian horsemen, where we began.

In crossing these countries to gather the images for this book, I have been struck by a characteristic common to all riding people: pride. Not the pride known in the West, which is nearer to vanity, but the true pride of a horseman, comparable to the pure self-respect of the horse, uniquely adorned with his saddle, arrogant without ostentation. 'A beautiful saddle adorns the horse like a beautiful wife adorns a home . . .' says one Mongolian song.

When the sun sets, at the moment when the mountains which border the horizon of the Gobi desert darken and take on a violet tinge, the Mongolian ancestor, one night, tethers his horse with its reins, crouches down, looks slowly at the countryside and says 'Man's heart should be like a saddled and bridled horse'.

THE SONS OF GENGHIS KHAN

The Mongols, or Tartars, as Westerners call them, are a people who conquered vast territories on horseback. Their place of origin, in what is today the People's Republic of Mongolia, was the common cradle of Turko-Mongolian invaders. Among the first of these invaders were the Hsiung-nu (about 300 B.C.-100 A.D.), the principal enemies of the Chinese dynasties of the Han and Chou, who during the sixth century ruled an empire which stretched from the Xing'an mountains to the Caspian Sea. However, no other army has left such an indelible imprint on the mass memory as that of Genghis Khan.

If you were to ask what was the secret power of the Mongolian army, we could say that primarily it was their weaponry: lightweight and close-fitting breastplates, powerful bows, battle-axes and maces, and siege engines. However, none of these arms would have been so decisively effective without the Mongolian horse. European thirteenth-century writers tell of the slenderness of the Mongolian horses, and were somewhat surprised by the minimal amount of attention these horses received (they were fed on grasses and straw, whilst the large horses of the Western World ate barley and oats), but above all the Europeans were amazed by their numbers. Not only did each rider have three or four mounts at his disposal, but the Mongol horde was followed by herds which provided fresh horses to be used while tired horses regained their strength. The horse wore leather armour made up of four pieces; two covering its flanks, one protecting its hind-quarters, and another its breast extending to the knees. Finally, the head was protected by a thin sheet of iron.

On the left: On horseback from a very young age, now, as in the past, the Mongols remain faithful to their history.

The horse depicted in religious art, on funeral stelae for example (Monastery of Ulan-Bator).

THE MONGOLS' TACTICS

Following the central Asian tradition, the Mongolian army had a decimal structure: ten units of ten soldiers made up a unit of one hundred, then of one thousand and then of ten thousand soldiers. This structure guaranteed strict discipline, which impressed the Europeans. In war the Mongolian army resorted to two tactics. The first involved deception. For example, the Mongols would lead their enemies into an ambush, surround them, and then descend upon them. When facing formidable forces, they made detours for one or two days and ransacked the region. If this was not possible they feigned a retreat for ten to twelve days, waited until the opposing army dispersed, and then returned to attack the country. The other tactics involved combat. The Mongols placed prisoners from defeated peoples at the centre of the front line, while their main force, deployed on the two flanks, surrounded the enemy and attacked. If their adversaries resisted, the Mongols slackened the encirclement, gradually let them disperse and then massacred them. It must be said, however, that the Mongols took great care to avoid close combat. They tried to bring down their enemies with showers of arrows, and approached only when they judged them to be sufficiently weakened. Retreat was part of their tactics and the long pursuits were always to their advantage because of their reserves of horses. The Mongolian army was without doubt most formidable in its skill in fighting in retreat; the archers firing as much over the back of the horse as over the front, re-deploying their strength and changing direction at will.

Thus, horses played a fundamental role in the art of war. Not only did they serve as mounts, but they also provided milk. Certain historians consider trading horses to have been as highly important in the time of Genghis Khan as nowadays. In *The Secret History of the Mongols* four out of five references to trading relate to breeding stock, the other relates to goats. Similarly in this book we find seven references to mare's milk, fermented and distilled, as well as two references to fresh mare's milk, although there is no mention of any other animal's milk or other dairy products. It is also worth mentioning that most of the Mongolian vocabulary relating to breeding is borrowed from Turkish, but any that refers to the horse is of an indigenous origin.

Today, horses retain all their importance in Mongolian life. Among breeding animals, they are con-

sidered as the most noble, and occupy a privileged place in the economic, social and ritual activity of the population. Horses are trained from the age of two, are made use of for four years, and at the age of six are considered to be at the peak of their strength, i.e., ready for long journeys. In the rather harsh climatic conditions of Mongolia, they rarely survive for twenty years.

A PREFERENCE FOR THE CANTER

The most characteristic technique of Mongolian horsemanship is the importance given to cantering, and we must say that this is well suited to the Mongolian way of riding, which is to place the saddle near the withers of the horse and lean forward. Since cantering is much less bumpy for the rider, it is judged to be more comfortable and less tiring. On the other hand Mongolian saddlery and riding technique seem more suited to archery than racing; even so, cantering allows the rider, standing upright in the stirrups, a surer aim. The Mongols train horses to canter by attaching them end to end. Some horses canter naturally and they are very much appreciated and are worth three or four times the price of an ordinary horse. Horse racing is categorized according to the type of horse: stallions, cantering horses, two-year-olds, three-year-olds, etc; but most popular with the spectators are the big races for horses over six years old. Mongolian horseracing is characterized by the length of the course, which is 30 or 60 kilometers, and by the age of the riders, who are six- to twelve-year-old girls and boys (it is the power of the horse that is in play, not the competence of the rider).

On the steppe, there are herds of many hundreds of horses made up, in fact, of families. Each family is led by a stallion, around which gather ten to fifteen mares with their colts and foals, as well as a certain number of geldings (horses castrated at three years of age). The stallions begin choosing their mares and starting their families at five years of age.

At home in the wild, the Mongolian horse required little food and stood up well to harsh climatic conditions. This facilitated his upkeep and allowed each horseman to have several mounts at his disposal.

Although domesticated, Mongolian horses are not as docile as Western horses. For example they never respond to a call. To catch them, a thin pole, about five metres long, weighing about four kilos and equipped with a rope loop, is used. The rider approaches at full speed and manipulates this loop with two hands, while at the same time clinging to the bridle at the saddle pommel. Horses that undergo special training are taught to stand firm with their front legs wide apart in order to save the rider from falling. Mongols ride only geldings. The stallions are used only for hunting wolves, and it is considered shameful to ride a mare. These customs were observed as early as the 12th and 13th centuries.

There are some preferences for the colour of the coat, and white seems to be considered the most prestigious colour. In effect, the Mongols relate colour to climate and the abundance of snow. In regions where the ground is reddish-brown with little snow, beige or reddish-brown horses are numerous. Therefore rulers or people of high status ride white or whitish horses. Mottled or mixed colours are avoided, and preference is given to single colours, with the exception of dappled grey, which is highly thought of.

On the following pages: The capture of animals was traditionally carried out with the aid of a long pole; at its end hung a loop, a lasso which could be passed around the neck and withers of the selected horse.

The modern Mongolian, far from disowning his history, has made his emblem the horseman of the steppe, galloping towards the rising sun.

A CHILD FOR A HORSE

The value accorded to horses explains the severity of punishments for their theft. Under the law of Genghis Khan, a thief had to replace the stolen horse with nine new similar horses. If he did not have the means to do so, he had to give up his child. If he had no children, he was slaughtered like a sheep. Among modern day Mongols, there seems to be a sort of national sport which is in reality stealing horses. This sport demands courage and competence and has its own rules. The main rule, and the most surprising, is the necessity to boast of your talents

as a thief, but you must never confess to having carried out a theft; otherwise you would be caught! The genuine thief does not steal in his home territory, but makes a long journey, boasting on the way of his power to steal the best horses from the herd of such and such a person in such and such a place, and it is only when he is sufficiently near the herd he is aiming for that he goes into hiding and puts to use his knowledge vis-à-vis the owner and his guards. If he is caught, he will be tortured. If he confesses, the owner can lodge a complaint with the authority under which the thief belongs, and he will be severely punished. If the thief does not confess, he will be set free and will enjoy the respect of all. Mongols say that there are some thieves so maimed by the tortures they have suffered that they are immediately identifiable as horse thieves, but they still manage to keep on stealing!

Left-hand page: The paradox of a country where modern times compete with the force of tradition and its obvious practical advantages; in broken terrain the horse is more useful than a motorcycle.

Mare's milk, like the traditional saddle, is not part of the past, but is still an important and beautiful part of daily Mongolian life.

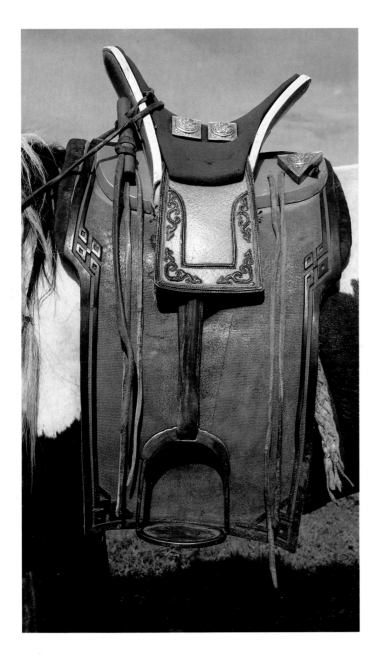

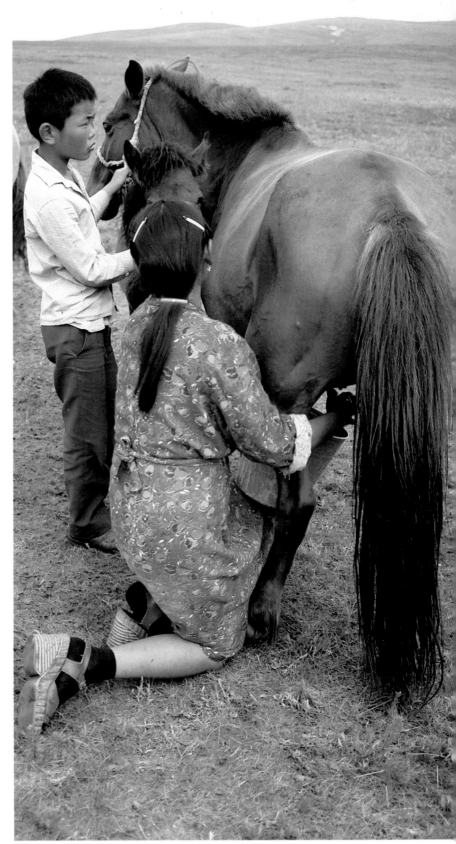

Up until the Revolution there was a strict division of labour according to the sexes. With some recent exceptions (notably trading), work with horses: herding, training and grooming, etc., was a man's job. This meant that women did not practice horsemanship and although they rode as well as men, more often than not their place on the back of a horse was exchanged for a place in an ox-drawn cart. This exclusion of females was not applied to other animals, and is proof of the special status given to the horse in Mongolian society.

Despite the construction of imposing temples, the majority of religious representations reflect the way of life of the nomad. This is illustrated by many statues of pack and transport animals.

Traditionally, the Mongols make use of the milk from their mares. Among the dairy products obtained from mare's milk, the most well-known to Westerners is airag or kumiss. The second name, of Turkish origin, is more familiar to foreigners. Kumiss is mare's milk which has undergone an acidic-alcoholic fermentation; the word airag is reserved exclusively for mare's milk, that is fermented naturally. As soon as the milk has been treated it is put into a goatskin bottle, or sometimes a wooden urn made for that purpose. These receptacles are always kept on the left-hand side of the entrance

Hunted or worshipped, the horse forms part of magical painted scenes, and also of ritual sacrifices (Museum of Ulan-Bator).

On the left: In the family yurt, an area is reserved for masculine activities, notably, the making of fermented milk.

into the yurt (a space reserved for masculine activities). Every day the Mongols pour in new milk for the day's consumption, thereby permitting a continuous process of fermentation during the production season. The receptacle must be shaken-frequently in order to obtain good alcoholic fermentation. The airag is considered to be a fortifying drink, above all rich in vitamins, and the Mongols consume great quantities of it. They also obtain a distilled alcohol from it.

The horse was used in sacrifices from antiquity to the Middle Ages. A Chinese document of the 13th century tells us that the slaughter of the horse was limited to special occasions. The consumption of horse meat was also rare at that time, but the introduction of Lamaism in Mongolia in the 16th century made this custom disappear completely. The horse is no longer slaughtered on ceremonial occasions or rituals, but airag is still considered an essential form of offering or purification, thanks to the ritual status of the horse in this society, and also undoubtedly because of its white colour. Thus, airag constitutes an offering of drink or food par excellence.

The art of horsemanship was mastered very early by the Chinese, as they created and used original methods. Thus the breast strap, for a long time not part of the Mediterranean harness, allowed rather small horses to pull wagons of impressive size. This scene, an extract of a chariot procession from the Hun era (206 B.C. — 200 A.D.), engraved in stone, shows a horse that is frisky despite the weight of two passengers in this vehicle with enormous wheels that it pulls.

CELESTIAL HORSES

The traveler roaming across Northern China can not help being struck by the great number of carts drawn by horses or mules that are seen on the roads. In about 1980, China counted about ten million horses, to which we may add just as many mules and asses. From this we are able to tell how important the equine species was in the daily life of the peasantry. Without travelling across the slopes of central Asia or into the Mongolian interior, our traveler will not meet anyone who could be called a horseman, since apart from military units and some national minorities, the Chinese do not ride horses. Or rather, they have hardly practiced horsemanship for a millennium.

THE CHARIOTS OF THE SHANG KINGS

The history of the Chinese horse starts more than three thousand years ago. The Shang kings, who ruled the Great Plains between 1700 and 1100 B.C., possessed chariots drawn by two horses, which they took with them into the afterlife in accordance with a custom common to the majority of peoples of that era who lived on the Eurasian steppe. Expert opinion varies as to where their chariots originated. A wild

The rich harnesses represented on these Chinese horses undoubtedly come from an early period when horses were used mainly for pulling vehicles, for all this material is very unsuitable to horse riding — as is the costume of the man who leads them.

Right-hand page: The importance given to the horse by the Chinese of the Shang period is clearly illustrated by the discovery of the remains of horses buried next to the bodies of their masters, and by numerous sculptures, executed with great skill.

horse, called a Prewalski, was abundant in a large part of ancient Chinese territory. It was a stocky animal, with short limbs, which the neolithic hunters took as game. However, it was only at the beginning of the second millennium that the inhabitants of the Great Plains started to breed horses. Archaeologists confirm that there are close resemblances between the chariots exhumed from the Hang tombs and prototypes from the northern Caucasus. There may well have been a simple transmission along the trails of Central Asia, but the method adopted for harnessing suggests invention, or at least local adaptation. Thus the horses pulling Hittite or Egyptian chariots of war were attached to the shaft by a supple collar which gripped their necks and slowed their pace; the small steeds of the Shang kings pushed forward by means of an intermediary horizontal belt, fastened to the shaft by a yoke, which covered them from the breast to the hindquarters. This original method of harnessing,

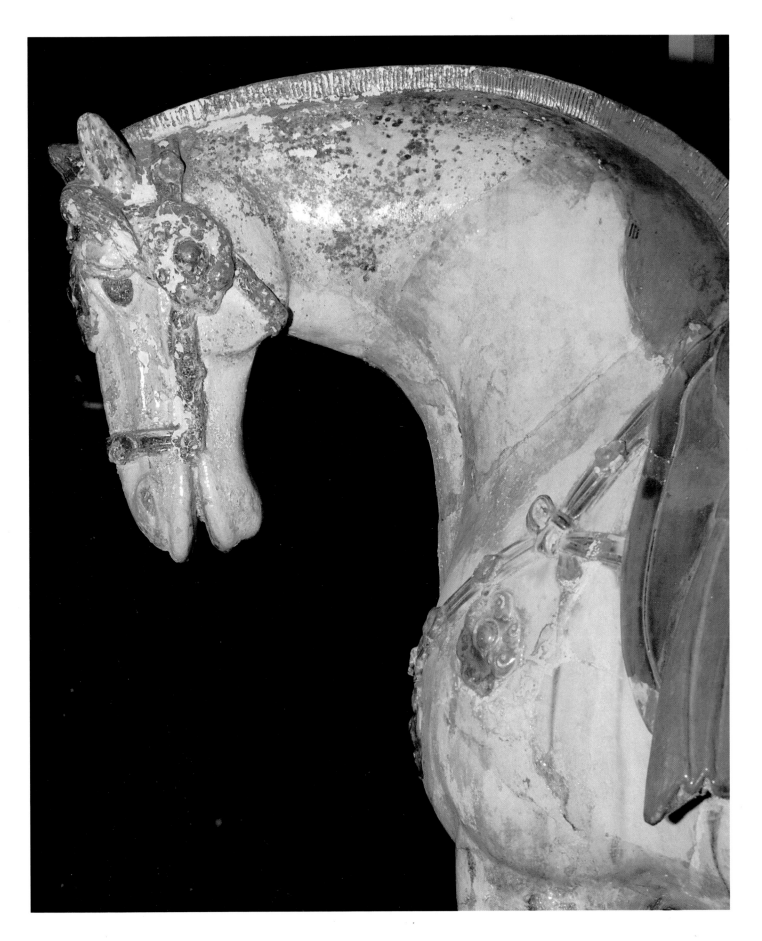

which could have derived from a technique perfected for oxen, assures the result, unknown by the classic Mediterranean cultures, of a more practical utilization of the animal's strength. This technical solution anticipated the perfection of the horse-collar, which appeared between the first and fifth centuries A.D. in the Far East. For over a millennium, the drawing of chariots remained the only way of using horses. The lightweight biga of the Shang made way for a high slung quadriga, adapted to cross-country warfare. From then on it carried three men, a driver with an archer on his right, and a warrior armed with a sort of halberd on his left. Horse dressage and chariot driving were thereafter classed above the martial arts and were a high priority in the education of young nobles. The horse was not only an instrument of combat. It played a part in every aspect of aristocratic life. It drew the chariots in which nobles paid visits to one another, and the richly adorned chariots in which betrothed women were conveyed to the residences of their future husbands. Each nobleman had to have his own expert in hippology, and all conversation revolved around this subject. (The Chinese vocabulary carefully distinguished between more than a dozen types of dress for charioteers.)

HORSEMEN OF THE WARRING KINGDOMS

It is very difficult to determine when horse riding began. Without doubt trainers had ridden horses for a long time. On the other hand, the abundance of garments worn by nobles restricted this type of exercise. Moreover, the vocabulary of the time refers explicitly to driving chariots; for example, the term bei, which refers to the reins, is written with a pictogram symbolizing a mouth fastened to a vehicle by two cords. Curiously though, the change over from chariots to cavalry does not seem, as in the ancient world, to have resulted from a sharp change in military technique; instead it corresponds with the end of an evolution which culminated in disaffection with the chariot. The warfare that the Chinese principalities indulged in during the first half of the first millennium was based on a highly ritualized

concept of combat. Chariots were maneuvered in formation and were accompanied by a badly-equipped infantry; the leading chariots launched the attack, clashed one to one and laid themselves open for whatever action ensued. It was considered in bad taste to exploit one's victories. As the feudal order developed into a very elaborate code of honour, warfare was transformed into a pure clash of force. Throughout the period of the Warring Kingdoms (480-256 B.C.), efficiency systematically caught up with ritual. Princes mobilized all the resources of their states and developed new tactics based on the infantry and fortifications. Numerous armed conscripts were sent into battle and the chariot was reduced to the role of transporting military chiefs. The Kingdom of Ts'ao, with close links to the nomads of the northwest, was a state situated in the present-day province of Yangtze, and it was to this region that historical accounts attribute the simultaneous adoption of the pantaloon, a piece of barbaric clothing, and horse riding, in around 350 B.C. The oldest known representation of a saddled horse comes from the mausoleum of the First Emperor, Huang-ti. Figurines of clay exhumed near the tumulus give the impression of a relatively archaic army. The bulk of the troops seem to be made up of infantry, heavily equipped with cross-bows and bronze halberds; heavy four-wheeled chariots seem to have been used as command vehicles. Nevertheless, there are several riderless horses carrying plate-armored saddles, without pommel or cantle, and which are fixed by a ventral belt.

THE QUEST FOR CELESTIAL HORSES

Having thus made a discrete appearance in the peripheral regions, horseback riding truly conquered China during the course of the Han dynasty (206 B.C.-220 A.D.). We can't really say that Liu Pang, the restorer of imperial unity, conquered the world on horseback, but there is hardly any doubt that, in the 2nd century B.C., it was the possession of large numbers of cavalry that made possible the extension of the empire's borders and the absorption of immense territories, as much to the south as to

Stirrups, saddle rug, crupper and bridle were the equipment of the Chinese rider and are very close to those used today by modern horsemen.

Towards the middle of the 2nd century B.C., a young officer by the name of Zhang Qian took the road west, with the mission of outflanking the Hsiung-nu to the south and establishing contact with their enemies in the west. Captured en route, Zhang Qian gave his captors the slip and travelled for many years through various kingdoms situated beyond the passes of the Pamirs. The recounting of his adventures germinated in the minds of the Emperor's advisers the idea of an alliance with the owners of the fabulous celestial horses, more prosaically the horse breeders of Ferghana. Methodically the imperial diplomats negotiated the purchase of stallions destined to improve the indigenous breeds.

Countless foals were born and at the turn of the first century B.C. the Chinese army was capable of lining up more than 200,000 robust chargers, which allowed for the launching of vast offensives. Central Asia was pacified up to and just beyond the Tarim. They had set out on the road to happiness. The sudden influx of Ferghana horses, — easily recognizable by their tall stature, long necks, and slender heads, — was the origin of a change in customs. Taller and above all more elegant than the local mounts, the new animal was made the object of true adoration. In contrast with the Prewalski horse, singularly absent in the art of the Shang and Zhou, effigies of the celestial horse multiplied. Mounted, walking, galloping or harnessed to a light barouche, this horse was ever-present. Moreover, it figured on the colossal bas-reliefs of the tomb of the general Huo Quping, the conqueror of Central Asia, as well as on the mosaics and mural paintings which adorned the tomb walls of the aristocracy. The dead took their escorts of miniature riders and carriages with them to the afterlife. These representations give us some idea of the progress that had been made in the art of horseback riding as well as in harnessing techniques; for example, the spread of the breastplate harness. Whether an indispensable instrument in the war against the nomads or simply an object of prestige, the horse was expensive. Military campaigns used so many horses that it reached the stage where, after the defeat of Liu Guangli in 90 B.C., the halt of operations in Central Asia could be attributed to the impossibility of replenishing the armies. Tax exemptions were offered to farmers with

the west, where the Chinese outposts bordered the Hellenistic world.

Alongside the unification of the agricultural world came the organization of the nomads. Various tribes of horse breeders among which the anthropologists identify proto-Turkish or Indo-European populations, formed a federation ruled by the war lords, the Shanyu, which Chinese geographers of the time generically named Hsiung-nu, and who were perhaps related to the Huns who surged into Western Europe at the decline of the Roman Empire. Faced with deadly raids by mounted archers straight from the steppe, the Chinese strategists had only one option: to adopt their enemy's tactics, using, if possible, faster mounts. Thereby began the prodigious quest for tianma, or celestial horses.

the aim of encouraging horse breeding, but nothing came of it. The farmers preferred cattle to horses which consumed great amounts of grain and fodder. This opinion was also reflected by the aristocracy themselves. Mural paintings depict land which is strictly segregated: cattle sheds for the field workers and stables for the masters' pleasure.

THE INVENTION OF THE STIRRUP

We have yet to discuss the conditions under which the stirrup appeared. From the 4th century A.D., the Chinese and their adversaries of the steppe both swapped their flat saddle for a saddle with a pommel and much heavier cantle, on the front of which hung iron stirrups. High up on the horse, the rider could make use of close combat weapons. Dunhuang paintings, from approximately the 5th century A.D., show us examples of a heavy cavalry reminiscent, several centuries later, of the elite troops of Byzantium. The knight, covered from head to foot by a long coat sewn with rings of metal, is literally welded to his mount, which is protected by a caparison. Without doubt these developments are not unconnected with the withdrawal of the Han State before the barbarian advance. For about three centuries (304-581 A.D.), the north of the country, carved up into short-lived kingdoms, completely escaped control by a central power and lived under the domination of small nomadic peoples such as Tibetans, Turks or proto-Mongols. The large Chinese families who stayed put adopted the morals and copied the ways of the nomads.

THE TANG AS HORSEMEN

There is some uncertainty as to the ethnic origin of the Li family who, at the turn of the 7th century, seized the throne and founded the Tang dynasty (618-907 A.D.). However, the question of whether

The Chinese today need all their arms — and all their hooves. The ancient hand-cart can not always be replaced by the motor vehicle. Happily, horses are there to take part in the national economic effort, as far as they can — as they have done for centuries in Europe. And even the West is rediscovering the advantages of animal traction for light work.

You mustn't conclude from the occasional posed photograph that the horse is merely quaint: Even if it is no longer a symbol of power, it really does play an active role in Chinese lives, and its place is much more important than that of a photographic subject for tourists.

they were Chinese immigrants, barbarians, or Turks is itself of little importance. In every respect the Tang, even more than the Han, were horsemen, whose art is a permanent glorification of man's most beautiful servant. Like the general Huo Quping, Li Shimin, founder of the Tang, placed effigies of his favorite steeds in his tomb. Statuettes in glazed ceramic, three colours, are so common that there is hardly a museum or a collector who does not have one. The celebration of horses, no longer the exotic celestial horses but the very uninspiring mounts resplendent in health with rounded hindquarters, were one of the major sources of inspiration for court painters. Representations of chargers fully harnessed and being ridden at tournaments and polo matches, not counting the more intimate scenes of horses being watered or rubbed down, were themes which were relentlessly repeated as much by the artists of that time as they were by artists in subsequent dynasties. During the Han era,

to ride a horse was above all a chance to display one's wealth. A young man from a good family could only be seen riding a horse of great value, and ladies, young and old, paraded on horses covered with resplendently colored saddle cloths, and with their feet hidden beneath voluminous pantaloons.

The capital Chang'an, despite having an immeasurable expanse of dozens of kilometers of avenues, could not be crossed on horseback or by mule. Moralists complained that noble families squandered money on their stables and kennels, buying grain and meat which rarely appeared on the tables of the poor. The government effectively sanctioned the expenditure of very important revenues to maintain the upkeep of the horse breeding establishments and the equipment of elite mounted troops. In the end the priority given to the cavalry proved to be a heavy burden, fraught with social consequences. From antiquity, but even more so after the military reforms imposed in 550 A.D. by the barbarian dynasty of the Western Wei, the rank and file of the army were recruited from the peasantry, who were dependent on their officers to pay for their equipment. At that time the cost of a horse and the complete equipment of a cavalry rider far exceeded the economic possibilities of even the most prosperous farmer. So, in order to make up the units of his guard, the emperor got into the habit of recruiting nomads, such as Turks or Iranians, who were paid in gold. Held only by the lure of profit, these mercenaries very quickly became an element which made for political instability. In 754 A.D., a mutiny led by a general of Turkic origin, An Lushan, put the dynasty in danger for the first time. Coups d'état and uprisings were an integral part of the political climate of the 9th and 10th centuries A.D. Whatever their real degree of loyalty, the cavalry was the only effective military force, and this was made obvious by the way in which, for example, the hordes of peasant revolutionaries who followed Huang Chao on his long march across the empire, carefully avoided the towns where cavalry units were garrisoned. In the end the budgetary cost of the cavalry was the cause of a rapid reduction in war strength. Towards the end of the 9th century, the government was reduced to making up units mounted on mules. At the beginning of the 10th century the Turkic Shatuo seized the capital with ease, using a contingent of 20,000 horsemen.

THE END OF THE GOLDEN AGE OF THE HORSE

With the Tang dynasty the golden age of the horse and the cavalry came to an end. Under the Sung (960-1279 A.D.) a compromise was reached whereby the Chinese empire made the populations of the steppes in the North and West responsible for raising horses used by the army and its outposts. Thus every year China imported a great number of beasts. In reality this system, generally described as tribute, put the Chinese government in a situation of extreme dependency. In addition it was compelled to assign an appreciable portion of the commercial surplus of silk and tea to the never ending demands of the nomads. During the Sung dynasty there occurred events that put the Chinese dynasties at the mercy of the invasions from the North. During three invasions, in 1125 A.D. by the Jurched, in the 13th century by the Mongols and in the mid 17th century by the Manchus, an apparently solid empire collapsed under the blows of a people one hundred times less numerous. Various elements can explain this fragility. One of the most convincing theses is the movement towards the south-east of agricultural and artisan production centres and the reorientation of commercial activity towards the great natural waterways and the sea. According to all the evidence, the north, less wealthy and less densely populated, already seemed to be an underdeveloped region. This relative weakness, which is not necessarily the sign of a decline, can nevertheless be related to the demise of the horse. Not that horses disappeared as mounts or no longer pulled vehicles; the utilization of the horse-collar, much earlier than in Europe, assured the improved efficiency of animal traction, without provoking any revolution in the transport of the economy; but although the horse retained a considerable military importance, it was, driven back to the margins of culture. A small example which reflects this transformation in mentality occurs towards the end of the 14th century, when a censor remonstrated with the emperor and the heir-apparent for having participated in a polo match! It was considered both undignified and dangerous for a sovereign to hoist himself into the saddle. The palanquin replaced the charger as the overt sign of power.

THE RIDERS
OF THE RISING SUN

In various regions of Japan remains of horses have been found which date back to the time when the archipelago was still attached to the Eurasian continent. However, there is no proof that these horses played a role in the life of the first occupants of the country, and indeed horses disappeared after the separation of the islands.

New traces appeared at the end of the Neolithic era (c. 9000 B.C.- 3000 B.C.), in the Jomon era, the period of pottery decorated with a cord pattern. The presence of horse bones among agglomerations of shells from about the 5th century B.C. suggests domestication, and that the horse may have been reintroduced from the Continent. The sites where these remains were discovered are scattered over the breadth of Japan, from Okinawa to Hokkaido, but are above all present in Kanto (a region near Tokyo).

Throughout the following era (second half of the 3rd century B.C. till the end of the 3rd century A.D.), called Yayoi and essentially characterized by rice growing, sites harboring the remains of horses were most numerous in western Japan. We then notice a clear increase in the average size of the horse, which is proof of efforts to improve the breed and, perhaps, cross-breeding with animals from the continent. We do not know much about how the horse was used in this period, but neither mare's milk nor horse meat seems to have been consumed and there is nothing to suggest the employment of the horse for agricultural

A code of honour, ritual gestures, and shining armour, irresistibly recall the age of chivalry. But in Japan, it lasted much longer than in Europe and, notably in the case of the harness, gave rise to art often more precious and more sophisticated, as much in the materials used as in the work itself.

work. Thus it is probable that it was raised more for display purposes than for practical use.

TERRA-COTTA HORSES

The late 3rd century A.D. until early 8th century A.D. is an obscure era which archaeologists describe as the period of great burials because of the existence of large tumuli (kofun) erected by the aristocracy, and which are normally separated into three periods. Throughout the middle period (5th — 6th centuries) we see a radical change which is at the origin of the theory of a civilization of the horse and which is identifiable by a number of artifacts such as pieces of harness, decorative objects in the form of a horse, terra-cotta figures (haniwa-uma) and mural paintings, etc. This sudden appearance of harnesses and representations of the horse is in striking contrast to their absence during previous eras. Certain pieces, such as saddle ornaments of gold-plated copper, wooden stirrups covered in iron, small bells of bronze, bridle bits made of gold-plated copper, resemble those of various Korean kingdoms and thereby suggest that these objects were imported. Furthermore, it is a fact that, later on, when harness production commenced in Japan, it was manufactured by naturalized Koreans.

Like the continental saddle, the Japanese saddle was made up of four pieces of wood; two saddle-trees and two plates with an interstitial space between them. This type of saddle, known from that period onwards as the kofun, survived in Japan until the introduction of the Western harness in the 19th century. As for the stirrups, these were fixed to the anterior part of the saddle, until they were moved towards the median part, and thereby were distinguished from the Chinese technique. Likewise they rapidly evolved from a ring shape into a hoof shape, specific to Japan.

THE EQUESTRIAN PEOPLES

The rapid spread of this equipment across the archipelago gave birth to the ingenious theory of equestrian peoples (kiba minzoku) in the mind of a Japanese archaeologist, Egami Namio. Although not supported by the majority of historians, this hypothesis throws new light on the origins of the Japanese state. Egami starts from the conquest of Korea, reported in Chinese historic sources, which was led by a 'king' named Ching Wang whose descendants, or successors, would have come across the Tsushima straits at the beginning of the 4th century. From the north of Kyushu, they would have progressed eastward and annexed the indigenous political centre (the Kyoto-Osaka-Nara region) by the late 4th century. The evidence for this theory is based on the similarity of myths of Japanese origin about the foundation of the league of Kaya in South Korea, the progression eastward by the imperial Japanese family and the foundation of Puyo and Koguryo. The imperial Japanese family would therefore have drawn on its tradition of horsemanship, preserving the customs and culture of the nomad warriors. Only the intervention of such a group could, in effect, explain the radical changes observed in the Japanese culture.

The main arguments put forward to support this thesis are as follows:

1. The transition was abrupt and can not be considered the result of spontaneous evolution, particularly if reference is made to the agrarian character of the Yayoi era and to the natural inertia of the rice growing populations;

2. A total correspondence between the Japanese equestrian civilization and the cultural forms of Korea and contemporary Northern China is observed;

3. The number of horses, of little importance in the previous era, increases phenomenally in the

middle of the Kofun era, which suggests that the equestrian peoples arrived in Japan with their horses;

4. The Japanese culture became seignorial and aristocratic, and its spread presupposes the conquest and domination of the country by force;

Whether it was a gold medallion or harness meant for the mounts of the Samurai, a pictorial art of exceptional quality, executed on silk or varnished wood, was developed in Japan. There the theme of free horses achieves a delicacy rarely equalled. Only an outline is necessary to suggest life and the horse is seen as the strength of the soldier and the supremacy of his emperor. Far from suggesting decadence, this beauty was created by a simple society troubled by incessant wars.

Following pages: It was relatively late that the horse played an important part in the Japanese warrior tradition. It was exclusively the mount of the leading Samurai; chariots were harnessed to oxen.

5. Many later tumuli of the period are built in strategic places;

6. In the long run, the sea has never been an obstacle to equestrian peoples.

Egami drew support for his argument from certain characteristics of the political organization, the method of imperial succession, and the status of women in the aristocratic families, as well as the role and the place of foreigners in the society. Egami's hypothesis nevertheless comes up against criticisms that are difficult to circumvent. In effect, Egami was searching for the origin of the imperial family of Japan among the peoples of Puyo. However, they were by no means horse-riding nomads, but rather agricultural people whose civilization resembled that of the farmers of the Yayoi era more than that of the nomadic horse breeders of Central Asia. It is therefore unlikely that they would have brought a complex culture of equestrian peoples from the north of the continent. The archaeological facts themselves do not add up. Remains of horses uncovered at the sites of the Kofun era are not superior in number to those of the Jomon and Yayoi eras. In addition most of the skeletons buried in the tumuli were those of old horses. This would suggest that horses enjoyed great care and attention, probably because of their rarity. Harnesses and figurines were more likely signs of foreign origin and the prestige attached to all things related to the horse. We must also take into account the absence of horse-drawn vehicles or chariots.

With regard to the historic documents, apart from the mention of horses in the mythological passages, it is above all the chronicle of *Nihon shoki* which teaches us about the role of the horse in the society of the time. The annals of the emperor Ojin (end of 4th century/beginning of 5th century) relate to the tribute of two horses offered by the king of Paekche; and those of the emperors Richu and Ingyo contain episodes in which horses play an unquestionable role. After the references which relate to the giving of horses by Japan to Paekche during the reign of the emperors Yuryaku and Buretsu, horse breeding might have reached a level whereby the formation of cavalry corps would be possible towards the end of the 5th century. However, no description highlighting cavalry battles is given before the Jinshin revolt (672 A.D.).

THE MOUNT OF THE GODS

If the imperial family is really of equestrian origin, it seems to have rather quickly lost the equestrian habit. From the 8th century, it was the ox-drawn carriage which was pre-eminently the aristocratic means of transport. The image of the hidden emperor concealed in a slow moving ox-drawn carriage, is far removed from that of the active rider. Besides, it was a new social stratum, the warriors or Samurai who much later achieved the status of horsemen. With few exceptions, only the generals of the infantry were mounted. As for the saber, adapted to cavalry combat, this only appeared in the 9th century.

Although the Japanese culture was not a civilization of the horse, in the era of internal peace imposed by the Shogunal dynasty of the Tokugawa (1602-1868), the equestrian tradition, though weakened even in the warrior class of the Samurai, retained a special place. On the one hand, the horse was used as a beast of burden for agricultural work, above all in the eastern part of the archipelago. On the other hand, it was considered a symbol of prestige. In the Tokugawa era, for example, a richly harnessed horse walked at the head of the cortege of a feudal lord, though he himself was transported more comfortably in a sedan chair.

Furthermore, horses fulfilled a ritual function. Horse races were religious events. The horse was the mount of the gods, and according to certain ethnologists, there might be a link between the sacrifices of horses and worship of the water spirits. In many respects, the relationship between Japanese civilization and horses remains a mysterious subject.

Many historic portraits feature the famous Samurai. The European imagination sees them most often on foot, but their princes and war chiefs were in fact mounted. And the costume of these officers appeared even more impressive when complemented by the trappings of the horse. Military techniques had to take account of cavalry; and so there were ceremonies and games for mounted archers dating from this period.

THE SACRIFICE

OF HORSES

THE HORSE IN BRAHMANIC CULTURE

The horse seems to have been introduced into India in the proto-historic era and to have been of Indo-European origin, at least as far as the rites with which it is associated are concerned. Although its provenance is difficult to pinpoint with certainty, it has been established that it was associated from Vedic times (c. 800 B.C.?) with the idea of territorial conquest and sovereignty, as well as with some deities.

A rare animal, which was imported at great expense and looked after with care, the horse is both one of the most valorous of sacrificial victims, a symbol of the sun, and the imperial mount. Its sacrifice (acvamedha; acva: horse) was the most costly, solemn, long lasting — a year or more — and the most exceptional, for it could only be offered by a sovereign of unquestioned authority over a vast territory, whose brilliant victories had testified to his power.

According to the sacred texts whose verbal composition goes back to the 7th-6th centuries B.C., the horse was the essential victim of the sacrifice. Each part of its body corresponded to a part of the Universe and Cosmic Time. The year, season, month, fortnight, days and nights were identified with its spirit (atman), and with parts of its skeleton. Its belly was the atmosphere, its back the sky, its eye the sun, its bones the constellations, the lower part of its abdomen the earth, its flanks the regions of

The famous equestrian columns of the temple of Sreerangam confirm the importance that the horse had in ancient India.

41

Above: The cosmic wheel and the horse; solar symbol and imperial mount, reunited according to tradition. Below: Only a powerful sovereign was allowed to organise the ritual sacrifice of the horse.

and his following set out on a trip which lasted a year. All the lands that they crossed were considered to belong to the king; it was a symbol of universal conquest.

During that year of peregrination, the sacrificial site was thoroughly prepared. It was vast. Pavilions were erected which, when the time came, would serve to shelter the king's wives, the sacred chariots, the officiants, the musicians, and all those who had a role to play in the final rite. Lastly, twenty-one stakes were planted firmly in the soil, to which would be tied the victims, who had to be immolated before the horse, as well as twenty selected animals, many of which had solar symbolism.

On the return of the horse, probably led by the noble young warriors who accompanied it, the sacrifice proper began and lasted for three days. There

space and its sides the intervening regions. In short, it encompassed the Cosmos. Its yawn is compared to a flash of lightning, its tremble thunder, its urine the rain and its breath the wind. In sacrificing the horse, the king identified with it, recomposing the great Cosmos in order to become its master.

AN EMPIRE MAPPED OUT BY HORSES

Consequently, everything was aimed at making that grandiose ceremony perfect. The horse was meticulously selected. It had to be young, beautiful in every way, and a fast steed; in other words, only a prize beast was judged worthy of being offered and identified with divinity. Then one hundred geldings were chosen, destined to make up its cortege, and four hundred young nobles were designated to follow it everywhere it went as well as to defend it against thieves or aggressors. On the appointed date established by the king's astrologers, the stallion

were offerings of food and drink, acts in the sacred fire and chants, etc. On the second day mares were presented to the horse, which incited him to neigh. Its neighing was considered the equivalent of a prayer chant; then it was harnessed with three other horses to the royal war chariot in which the king took his place, leading it towards a pool to the east of the sacrificial site. When the chariot had returned to the altar, the four principal wives of the king dressed the horse's mane and tail.

THE RITUAL SACRIFICE OF THE HORSE

The victims tied to the stakes were then slaughtered, except for the horse which, after having been untethered and led to the north of the site, was strangled. The royal wives honored it with a triple circumambulation, whispering words of love to it and simulating a coupling with it, which was an allusion to the rite of fecundity. The horse and the other animals were then cut up with a knife and, later in the night, there was a communal tasting of the flesh thus sacrificed.

On the third and last day was the solemn oblation of the sacred liqueur, soma, a nocturnal vigil marked by ritual recitations, chants, and music which would conclude the grand sacrifice that had consecrated the king as universal sovereign or chakravartin, (he who makes the Wheel turn, chakra, an implication of the law of dharma).

Finally, the fourth day was reserved for a purifying bath taken collectively in the nearby pool, or river, before everyone returned home. Substantial offerings were distributed by the king to the officiants, and the people considered themselves to be associated with his glory and the prosperity of the kingdom.

In this important era, figurative art still did not exist; at least none has survived to our times. Only the texts describe this imperial sacrifice where the horse plays the all important role. On the other hand, lapidary inscriptions attest to the execution of this rite by kings wishing to make known their supreme power. However, we should note that these monarchs were not Buddhists. The first Indian em-

Hindu iconographic tradition has always associated the horse with great divinities, such as Durga, symbol of feminine energy.

perors, the Maurya, did not use the horse sacrifice. However, the founder of the following dynasty, that of the Counga, celebrated it; he was a usurper general called Poushyamitra, who reigned from 187 to 151 B.C. and who makes mention of two acvamedha in that period, which marked the beginning of a Brahmanic reaction against Buddhism.

It is in the same religious context that two of the sovereigns of the Gupta dynasty, equally Indian and Brahmanic, carried out this imperial rite: Samudragupta (335-*circa* 375 A.D.) who boasted of having restored it, and Kumaragupta I (c.414-*circa* 455). The first of the two had himself represented on his coinage, notably in gold, in front of a horse beside a stake. This theme was the epitome of that of the universal sovereign, the chakravartin which had figured in the Buddhist iconography in a more complete form (we will meet with it again further on).

THE EXTENSION OF THE RITE

These Rajput miniatures show the richness of their harness, and therefore, the attention paid to horses; for it was considered vital for the sovereign to prove his wealth and his strength in this way.

From the Gupta era, and probably before, the imperial sacrifice of the horse seems to have lost a little of its exceptional character. Up until then, it was the sign of a conqueror who wished to be universal and bring together the populations over which he exercised his authority. The extent of the territories dominated by the Counga was not equal to that of the Maurya dynasty, and the same celebrated king held two acvamedha during his reign instead of one,

with the acknowledged aim of consolidating his conquests a second time, before bequeathing them to his son and successor. Under the Guptas, who were nevertheless very powerful monarchs and the originators of a sort of golden age in the Indian world, we see a vassal dynasty — besides that connected to the Guptas by marriage — that of the

The harness pictured, considered to be that of Krishna, changes little in the numerous representations of it, and demonstrates that this equestrian technique was familiar to horsemen throughout India (School of Kangra).

Vakataka (from 300 to *circa* 500), performing the same rite. Two of their kings carried out this ceremonial ten and four times respectively. It was perhaps necessary in this case to show a certain ostentation: they were a very rich family who could pride themselves on their alliance with the emperor. But it was also the sign of the extension of this rite to local sovereigns, and therefore also of the loss of the notion of a universal monarch.

The sacrifice of the horse is still mentioned in the second half of the 7th century. The last one seems to have been celebrated in the 9th century, in Orissa. However, for all that, its existence was not forgotten and the epic literature, of which the *Mahabharata* is the most well-known example, perpetuated it, to the point where certain miniatures in the Mughal style (17th century) depict it, from later and corrupted versions.

45

The symbolic importance accorded to the horse from the Vedic age is echoed in later mythology and religious iconography. Many gods and goddesses have a horse for a mount: the sacrificial Fire, Agni; the Dawn, Usas; the Sun god, Surya and Vishnuin his ultimate incarnation as Kalki, etc. These horses are sometimes personified by a proper name and very often associated with the notion of sacrifice. The horse which Vishnu/Kalki mounts plays a major role. He has to lead the god over the land of men to the end of the Kali Yuga, that is to say the current period — which is that of war and worldwide disruption — in order to restore virtue. The horse is thus the major instrument of that Messianic aspect, the redeemer, which we find in Buddhism.

The horse is the privileged companion of the Maharajah, for whom hunting is the favorite pastime in times of peace.

THE SOLAR HORSE

It is undeniably in the iconography of the Sun god Surya that the presence of the horse is most constant; and from all the evidence it is put there in close harmony with the solar character of the god, who appeared in an anthropomorphic aspect in a relatively late period, towards the II-I centuries B.C., when he was one of the most revered gods of the Vedic times, but in his natural form or in that of a wheel, symbol of the sun.

He figured on the reverse side of coins issued both by the Indo-Greek kings who reigned in Bactria (northern Afghanistan), and by the Kushana sovereigns who dominated a great empire which embodied the current north of India, Pakistan and Afghanistan. And, curiously, he is figured sitting or standing on a royal chariot pulled by seven horses, just like Apollo in ancient Greece. Surya himself also symbolizes the path of the sun in space, and his galloping horses draw him from dawn to dusk in the sky. Another Vedic god, Agni, the fire of sacrifice, did the same if one is to believe the *Mahabharata* which describes him driving a chariot drawn by seven horses of red (evoking the flame).

It very much seems as though the anthropomorphic Surya of historic times brought together several related themes, and that he united the Indian view with the Greek conception. It is, if we wish to explain it another way, the synthesis of Indo-European notions, easily understood by the illiterate masses spread over the immense Eurasian territories, where the horse had acquired an undeniable sacrificial, solar and even cosmic character. This brief outline is based on innumerable examples, descriptions, rites, beliefs, interpretations, and hypotheses.

Furthermore, the iconography associated with Surya mounted on his chariot drawn by horses was originally much influenced by Hellenic Iran, a vast area where the horse was most valued and most utilized, from where it was brought the most often to India, and where the sun cult was personified by a god whose costume, manifestly of Western origin, differed completely from the traditional dress of the Indians. He wore a well-cut, sewn tunic with long sleeves (instead of the draped loincloth and nude torso), riding breeches and boots. This clothing

would have been unbearable in the suffocating heat of the Indian seasons. It was evidently a theme imported from the region situated to the northwest of India which spread throughout the northern part of the country without crossing the tropic of Cancer. But it seems that it met with an Indian tradition, perhaps more ancient, explained in the Books I to VII of the *Rig Veda*, where Surya is described driving a chariot drawn by a horse or even seven red horses (like those of the sacrificial Fire Agni).

In the regions of Afghanistan, the western type of Surya persisted long after the era of the Indo-Greeks and Kushana. Integrated into the Buddhist iconography we still see at Bamiyan (6th or 7th centuries) and he also appears in the Khair Khaneh (possibly 7th century) in a style related to that of Kashmir. However, making our way toward the centre and the east, the theme gradually loses its foreign characteristics: horses persist, but are sometimes treated in a rather aberrant way, and the only part of the costume that remains are the boots, to

attest to the role of the cavalier or warrior of god.

It is in this way that the iconographic theme has perpetuated itself for more than a thousand years and has won, step by step, kingdoms situated some 1500 kilometers from the place where it seems to have started. Among the consecrated temples of Surya, one of the latest and biggest was built in about 1250 at Konarak. It is a majestic construction, sadly partly ruined, situated in Orissa not far from the shore of the Gulf of Bengal. It represents an immense chariot with twelve wheels, drawn by seven horses with opulent caparisons, in which the god, wearing high boots, stands upright whilst riding one of the steeds. In the courtyard which surrounds the buildings is a wonderful group of sculptures in the round (which at another time flanked the south

47

door of the surrounding wall) representing a horse accompanied by a warrior. Trampled under his two front hooves is an unknown demon. It is a powerful work, worthy as much for its dynamic movement as for the accuracy of its proportions.

Whilst the ancient sculptures have brought few modifications to the Surya style conceived in northwest Pakistan and Afghanistan, we see them progressively Indianized from the classic period onward. Its Western costume is replaced by a nude torso decorated with jewels and a draped, close-fitting loincloth. On the other hand, the stylized evocation of the chariot drawn by fiery steeds lasts for a long time, the chariot being the most common engraving on the bases of the statues.

Progressing towards southern India (from about the 7th century on), Surya ended up completely integrated with the Indian style of other gods: his boots from then on disappeared, his feet were bare, and his chariot — and therefore his horses, no longer represented.

In this way an image, more than a thousand years old, which united numerous followers around a solar cult, and conquered people for whom the horse symbolized the essence of the solar journey through the Cosmos, faded away.

HORSES OF WAR

Irrespective of mythical horses of the Sun god Surya, war horses or display horses are hinted at in the epic literature. They are sometimes depicted on the reliefs decorating the Brahmanic temples, for example in the very long frieze which circles the basement of the temple dedicated to Lakshmi, in the famous site of Khajouraho (first half of the 11th century). Always represented in profile and walking, they have an aquiline nose, a simple harness, a saddle cloth and surcingles (a folded strap), in which their riders put the points of their toes,

The mixed heritage of the traditional Indian cavalry and the British military culture. A dignified squadron of Bengal Lancers marches to commemorate Republic Day in New Delhi.

दुरगदसकरनोत

The influence of the Arabic cavalry is very clear in a number of Indian equestrian pictures, as is seen in this Sikh painting, the step and the grey coat of the horse (despite the more rounded morphology), and the weapons of the rider are all of Arabic origin.

is interesting to recall that the horseman is also represented in the game of chess, which probably originated in India (5th century), and which was introduced into Europe by the Arabs in the 8th — 9th centuries.

In fact, the Moslems, according to various sources, were at the doors of India from the end of the 8th century, but were not yet threatening and were content to trade and make a few raids without mounting large offensives.

For many centuries the different Hindu kingdoms continued to develop, warring with one another, forming and dissolving political and military alliances, becoming stronger or decaying, celebrating their victories and their power with religious traditions ever more vast and sumptuous.

However, the Islamic wave broke across Northern India from the beginning of the 11th century with, this time, a precise objective: territorial conquest. Their advance was slow, but the Hindu kingdoms, prisoners of their traditional forms of warfare, were not able to coordinate a collective resistance quickly enough and were forced to surrender one after the other. The last to be attacked, those of the South did not capitulate until 1565 at the battle of Talikota.

THE EMERGENCE OF DOMESTICATED HORSES

It was in the 15th and 16th centuries that the theme of the monumental domesticated horse was used for the last time in some great Brahmanic ensembles of the south: in Conjeeveram (Kanchipuram) in the 15th century; at Velour in the 16th century; and above all at the temple of Ranganataswami at Crirangam (State of Madras) at the end of the 16th century, at the same time as the kingdom of Vijayanagar had been forced to capitulate before the Mogul invaders. These horses, eight in number, decorated the pillars of the Sesharayar Mandapa situated in the fourth enclosure, on the eastern side. Superbly caparisoned, mounted by riders brandishing swords, threatening predators overhead killed by the intrepid hunters, the horses of Crirangam strongly evoke medieval horsemen from the court of Vijayanagar, and the turmoil of royal hunts echoed in

stirrups only appearing at a later date. These are the traditional horses which, for many centuries, made up one of the four bodies of the royal or imperial army, and which participated as such in the strategy of war before the intervention of the artillery used by the Europeans and Arabs. Here it

descriptions of that time. We can see there, without undermining the grandeur or the ostentation, the gallantry of the Hindu sculpture, which henceforward became increasingly more decadent.

The horse does not altogether lose its mythical and guardian characteristics in popular tradition. We still find that in some years, in certain regions of southeast India, there are villages where every family has clay horses made by potters, which will be deposited in the ground near the settled area, and to which offerings are made. In return, the villagers can count on tranquil nights, sheltered

The numerous successful introductions of foreign horses has allowed the Indian continent to promote the development of several breeds, with different characteristics. Thus the horse, by his coat, his step or some morphological characteristic, allows his rider to stand out in popular social gatherings. (Pushkar Fair.)

The horse in India as everywhere, is linked to the family and the festival. Choosing it, acquiring it, dressing it, riding it . . . Taken to the fairs, it is man's greatest pride. And to judge a mount in the glimpse of an eye is considered a gift of god and proof of sagacity and experience. (Pushkar Fair.)

from incursions of thieves or brigands; for, according to tradition, they hear in their dreams a reassuring cavalcade. And, during the day, the pottery horses, although once again inert, reassure them, by their presence alone, that they are able to go about their business without fear.

The Horse in Buddhist Culture

From Buddhism, thanks to narratives and popular literature, we learn a great deal about the role of the horse in Indian Society.

A king headed the government, and noblemen made up the ruling class. As protectors of State security, it was these nobles who used horses, but the king owned the most beautiful steeds. Little is known except that the king was inclined to pay a fortune to acquire them, and princes, dignitaries and nobles were prepared to do the same as far as their means would allow.

Over many centuries, horses were imported into India from the plateaux of Upper Asia, Afghanistan and Eastern Iran. Every year, in the dry season, horse traders set out at the head of contingents of about five hundred beasts; they were preceded by an experienced guide who knew the route and its ambushes well, and they were also accompanied by professional grooms. All along their slow and perilous journey, they stopped in caravanserai, making detours in order to present their beasts in the most reputed palaces. The benefits of this seasonal operation could be considerable for the horse dealers as well as for the grooms who were assured of been engaged by the new owner in order to care for the horses which they had convoyed. Several accounts tell of the detestable habit that certain dishonest horse dealers had of stealing the best and most expensive animals, which they had previously sold, and then reselling them further on.

THE HORSE IN SOCIETY

Acquired for an exorbitant price, and needing specialized personnel, who were difficult to recruit on the spot, the horses were not all classed in the same category. In royal or princely stables there was the charger of the monarch, the remounts, and the sort of horses destined to be harnessed to chariots of war. As part of their owners' treasure, it was not unusual to see the horses used as gambling stakes when, as a last resort and desperate to win, players put them up as security, just as they did their jewels or their real estate.

A strict hierarchy was observed among the horses. Those which were trained for war had a proper name (like the elephants). Before being ridden into battle, they were drugged with wine. As a mobile element of withthe army, they were used for reconnaissance, hand fighting, the pursuit of fugitives and the taking of enemy reserves. Each royal dignitary and his followers provided their own contingent of horses, which were added to the royal herd. All were mounted by lancers, archers or swordsmen, and some were dressed in armour.

In peacetime, the horses were carefully looked after by the grooms and their helpers, who prepared their fodder, made up of barley, peas and oats, and carefully swept out the stables. Other minor staff included the untouchables (outcasts, because of working with animal carcasses), leather workers making the harnessing and English style saddles (5th to 6th century) as well as repairing damage sustained in combat; other artisans mended the arrows reclaimed on the battle field.

THE THIRD OF THE SEVEN JEWELS

All these horses, valuable as they were, did not equal the first among them: the thoroughbred of exceptional quality that only the king rode. It held, like the other royal mount, the elephant, the same rank as the state. In other words, it was the living symbol of the security of the kingdom in all circumstances where it could be threatened.

Here we find, in another form, the idea of the horse being linked to royal or imperial greatness, which it also symbolized in the Vedic acvamedha sacrifice. In the Buddhist milieu the horse was not put to death, but was associated with the universal royal person, that of the chakravartin, and, as such, it figured among the seven jewels of the sovereign of the world, which are carefully detailed and often represented on bas-reliefs of the ancient era of Buddhist art: the wheel, the elephant, the horse, the pillar (cosmic), the principal wife, the son-prince-heir apparent, and lastly the royal minister-advisor.

Whilst the women sleep, Prince Siddhartha (who is to become the Buddha Shakyamuni) flees from his home with his faithful steed Kanthaka. This horse and the groom Chandaka are to be the only witnesses of the 'Great Departure' of their master. (Guimet Museum, Paris.)

If it seems strange at this point to develop the hypothesis and comment on this theme, it should be remembered that the horse and the wheel (chakra) have been integrated into the iconography of the Buddha himself.

In fact, the Buddhist recitals relate to the rebirth of the Bodhisattva Siddhartha as a thoroughbred in several of his previous lives. One of them is the object of an illustration, drawn on an ivory plaque exhumed in the archaeological excavations made at Begram in Afghanistan (3rd century), and conserved in the museum of Kabul. Like many of the same species, the young stallion was led into Northern India by a horse dealer. However, because of several mishaps, the horse dealer, instead of selling it, gave it away to a humble village potter, who was perplexed, for he did not really know how to use the young horse. But he was not counting on the intelligence of a bodhisattva who mysteriously involved his destiny with that of a horse of the State. The worries of the potter were unfounded, and every-

thing worked out well for him. The thoroughbred of the king of Benares (currently Varanasi) had recently died and the ministers were in search of a stallion fit to succeed him. The horse-bodhisattva, who spoke the language of men, persuaded the potter to sell it very dearly, which was done, and it was led in all haste to the palace. Once lodged in the stables, the thoroughbred immediately embarked on a hunger strike. Very alarmed, the king came to visit it and the horse explained that he had not been received with all the honors due to his rank. This situation was immediately rectified in full by a ceremony which lasted seven days.

In several versions, these texts described the State horse so well that sculptors have also portrayed it.

The place of the horse is always high in the Indian hierarchy, and royal stables here are among the best run in the world. Here, in Jaipur, we see Maharani Gayatri Devi, with a few of her favorite horses, being led by hand in the gardens of the stud farm.

from the plateaux of Upper Asia and it was later adopted by the Indian grooms, at least for a time.

It occupied a stable decorated with purple and gold lambrequins. The royal groom would place a saddle cloth on his back, the golden harness around him, adjust the brow-band ornate with a plume on his head and braid his tail and on grand occasions, a golden sheath was added. As for the groom, he wore (like the god Surya in his septentrional/northern version) a longsleeved jacket, tailored and embroidered with a straight neckline and edged with gold braid; his legs were wrapped in breeches and he wore leather sandals on his feet: this costume was worn by men of the North convoying horses

THE COMPANION OF BUDDHA

The most famous horse in the Buddhist tradition is that of the prince Siddhartha, who became the historic Buddha Shakyamuni. Named Kanthaka, he was born, according to the legend, on the same day as his master, as well as those who were going to care for him and the royal groom-riding master Chandaka. Both this master and the horse were to be participators and spectators of a crucial event in the human life of the Buddha, i.e. his ultimate incarnation on this earth, which is called the Great Departure. This event was also important because it marked the break of the future monk of the Shakya from the princely life which he led from his birth in his father's palace. Having resolved to abandon this easy and protected existence, during which great care had been taken to spare him the knowledge of illness, old age and death, the prince Siddhartha ordered his riding-master in the middle of the night to go and saddle his horse so that he could leave the palace without anyone's knowledge.

Kanthaka let out a long and sad neigh, but he was promptly harnessed and the gods held up his hooves in order to muffle the noise and the riding-master ran ahead of the horse and his august rider, holding in his right hand the chakra, a formidable throwing weapon consisting of a large metal ring with a very sharp outer edge, capable of cutting off from a distance the head or a limb of potential assailants. This weapon (which still exists in the panoply of the Sikhs) is similarly one of the attributes of the god Vishnu, the god who travels through space, like the Sun.

When the future Buddha was far enough away from the palace, he ordered his horse and his riding master to stop. He set foot on the ground, he lay aside his finery and his sword and gave them back to Chandaka to be returned to his father, and he cut his long hair, put on a religious robe and was going to leave when the horse Kanthaka bent his front legs in order to kneel before him, licked the feet of his master while shedding burning tears. The legend specifies that he died shortly after his return to the royal stable and was born again among the gods. The touching scene of farewell of the royal horse figures in the repertoire of sculptors of Gandhara (today Pakistan), who were often more prolific than the Indian artists when it came to the iconography of the Buddha. Nevertheless, the Great Departure is handled with more skill in the Indian styles, particularly in the schools of the southeast (2nd-4th centuries).

BALAHA, THE WHITE HORSE

The bodhisattva, who was to become the historic Buddha Shakyamuni, was incarnated in another marvelous horse, with a white coat, who flew without wings. It was Balaha, whose history, reviewed and corrected by legend, is linked to the island of Sri Lanka (Ceylon). In fact, the plot of this story is utilized on many occasions in other episodes of previous lives of the Buddha. It is that of the shipwreck of a trading boat captained by the son of a rich Indian businessman, who has, no doubt, experienced adventure many times, and who is often evoked in literature, but the details which are inserted into this plot are special. The shipwrecked are welcomed with open arms onto an island populated by beautiful young women who shower them with caresses and charming attention. They are in

Following pages: The great horse market at Tilwara, in Rajasthan, is one of the most important gathering places of its type in India.

The prince of Wankaner-Gujerat shows here a Kathiawar horse, recognizable by the points of its ears which touch, and descended from Arab horses washed ashore after the shipwreck of trading vessels.

reality abominable ogresses who totally fool the sailors and imprison them in a fortress, while reserving the right to devour them all at their leisure and fulfill to their hearts' content their monstrous appetite.

Only the young captain resists their wiles and secretly plans his escape. Having managed to convince some of his companions to join him, he leads them to the shore where, miraculously, a gigantic white horse appears; it is Balaha, who comes to the island once a year and cries (for he is gifted with speech): 'For those who wish to return to India I will cross the sea'. As soon as the men cling onto his tail and mane, the divine horse rises into the air with its unusual load, flies over the ocean, and brings back the escapees to their homeland.

The horse of the future Buddha, dying shortly after the departure of its master and being reborn among the gods, has lent his prestige to the breed: here the presentation of a Kathiawar, recognizable by the pointed and curved ears.

On his return, the captain quickly assembles an imposing army and returns to Ceylon in order to wipe out the ogresses, and with the hope of liberating those of their prisoners whom they have not yet crunched between their beautiful teeth.

The story ends, naturally, with the victory of the young heroes, who associate their triumph with the horse Balaha, who is, despite appearances, the principal figure of that previous life. It is Balaha, the true Saviour, the Messianic bodhisattva, who by the accumulation of charitable acts towards all beings throughout his rebirths, attains the supreme state of Buddha (in this case, the Buddha Shakyamuni). This incarnation of Balaha, flying horse, is bound up with distant and various traditions in the regions of the steppe, notably that of Altar, where they were for a long time perpetuated in the body of Shamanism.

In the Buddhist iconography of ancient India, the story of the horse Balaha figures, among others, in the Mathura school of art, in an abridged version in three vertically superimposed reliefs on the inner wall of a stoupa balustrade (c. 2nd century) or, more completely, at Ajanta, in a mural painting of the 5th-6th centuries).

THE HORSE, BRINGER OF HOPE

With the evolution of Buddhism, an evolution slow and sometimes almost imperceptible, the theme of the flying horse, Saviour of men, transformed from the bodhisattva personifying the future Shakyamuni into the great bodhisattva Avalokiteshvara, an abstract entity, the bringer of great hope and the object of ardent veneration in all dangerous circumstances. In other words, the believers in Buddhism in the ancient form redirected their devotion onto this entity, renowned in later Buddhism as being a powerful resource in times of distress.

It is in this way that we find the horse Balaha integrated into a curious architectural ensemble erected in Cambodia, in the Angkor group, and consecrated in 1191 by the last great Khmer king Jayavarman VII (1181-1218). It is a small Buddhist sanctuary, designed by the Khmers in the name of

Neak Pean (the intertwined serpents) the symbolism of which is very complex, an imprint of religious ideas directly taken from India. Built at the centre of an artificial circular island, it is itself situated in the middle of a lake, also artificial, which is contained within sandstone walls arranged in a quadrangle. It is said to represent the home of the gods at the heart of the lake Anavatapta, traditionally situated in the Himalayas, and which escaped the destruction of the world. The waters of the Anavatapta are reputed to be curative and, by analogy, many faithful to them come to immerse themselves in the ornamental lake of Neak Pean, a replica of that cosmic lake. In the water, facing the eastern entrance and a modest landing stage, stands a great sculpture modelled in the round, cut from

Despite the legend of Balaha, the flying white horse, incarnation of the Bodhisattva, horses with darker coats are no less prized in India. Of course, a white horse is appreciated, but it is essentially its physical constitution which counts in a sale: the conditions of life (climate and ground) are very hard for the horse.

several assembled blocks: it is, once again, the horse Balaha, incarnation of Avalokiteshvara, the compassionate lord, who gallops across the primordial ocean, with men clinging to its tail, and lays them down in the divine residence, having protected them from the torments of mind and body.

THE PONIES OF

THE HIMALAYAS

THE EIGHT MASTERS
OF THE HORSE

The Buddhism which was taken up officially from the 7th century in Tibet is that of the Mahayana. It was incorporated into a local religion, the Bon, which previously existed in that region. Popular beliefs were maintained and, an amalgam resulted. Nevertheless, when the Bon had gradually con-

In the high valleys of Ladakh, ponies are still the best means of communication with the outside world.

Below: Ancient statuette from the monastery of Likkir, in Ladakh.

the definitive departure of the king's chaplain: 'The horse neighs; he is overwhelmed with pain; large tears as big as eggs fall from his eyes'.

On the other hand, in the technical and complex texts of the Buddhist and Bon theogony, the horse manifestly plays a dual role: cosmological and protective. Despite great variance in the later iconographic repertoire, a quite widespread constant can be seen: the horse (white, grey or, sometimes, black) is the mount of the guardians of the eight regions of space, called the eight masters of the horse, as well as of their leader, Vaicravana, who reigns over the southern part. This aspect is also an attribute of the transcendent Buddha (Jina) Ratnasambhava, who possesses a horse in the naming of his characteristics and, as a symbol, the jewel (ratna). The image of the horse transporting the jewel on its saddle is very well known. In popular Lamaist art, it decorates banners which are considered to bring good luck.

Many secondary divinities also are horses or riders. They are reputed to be the protectors of both the esoteric tradition of the Bon, transmitted verbally, and the lives of devout Buddhists, saving them from various impediments and annihilating their enemies, just like the great Bodhisattva Avalokiteshvara (who became the divine patron of Tibet), whose name only has to be repeated in litany in order to be free from all danger.

The horse is rare in the religious iconography of Tibet. Certainly it is still present in the Buddhist pantheon, but with much less than in India or Nepal.

THE HORSE FOR ALL SEASONS

In the popular beliefs and acts which define daily, family and seasonal life, the horse holds a special place. At least it did so up until 1959, the year when the Dalai Lama went into exile in India.

Before that, the horse was strictly associated with individual and collective life. For example, time was set in a twelve-year cycle, each year being designated by an animal symbol, and the horse was that of the seventh year of the cycle, which became part of the horoscopes which forecast the smallest of events. Furthermore, the house was protected by secondary divinities, of which the god of saddlery (created because of a dream, in which an unsaddled horse was mounted, which was determined to be harmful). At the time of a marriage, the nuptial

verted to the Buddhist religion imported from India, they maintained a certain orthodoxy because of the activity of successive reformers.

However, with regard to the important place held by the horse in the life of India proper, it must be noted that here in Tibet it was more difficult to identify. In the domain of the religious iconography, it is rarely the star of the show; the figure in the episode of the Great Departure is well known, but is presented without Kanthaka's emotional farewell to his master, which the works of India and Gandhara (Pakistan) reflect. However, this episode is often evoked in epic literature throughout the period described, with the help of almost identical terms,

procession got under way at dawn. It was led by a man dressed in white, mounted on a white horse and solemnly carrying the horoscope of the newly-married couple, who followed both him and the horse. At harvest time celebrations, horseraces took place and these helped in the threshing of corn, according to a custom found in many civilizations: tethered to a central axis, they went around treading the sheaves of corn spread out on the ground, in order to separate the grain from the chaff.

Horseraces were organized for all the grand-celebrations, notably for the new year. They included, in some circumstances, jousting competitions in which riders set off at full gallop and had to try and pierce a target with an arrow or a lance. This was notably the case in the celebration of the admission of a young official to his job.

Relics of times past — perhaps now disappeared — from a Buddhist society in which the ruling class was descended from horsemen skilled in war and hunting.

The guardians of the eight regions of space, also called 'the eight masters of horses', have horses as their mounts in the texts; during festivals these figures which represent them remain seated

THE MOUNTS OF
THE CONQUERORS

On the Iranian plateau and in neighboring regions, the horse is in one of its original environments. Here, its domestication occurred earlier than elsewhere and its utilization, more thoroughly pursued, destined it above all for hunting and warfare. Very early on the horse was considered as one of the major elements of military tactics, whether offensive or defensive, and for a long time it was an undeniable technical advantage over contending forces still ignorant of the equestrian art.

The history of these regions is made up of almost permanent conflict between the sedentary population and the nomadic invaders. It is a succession

In the confines of Kashmir, transport is still often on the back of a small horse (left-hand page), as in Iran five centuries B.C.: above, this bas-relief (north staircase of the Apadana, Persepolis) shows the giving of a horse, a most beautiful present for the Persian sovereign.

of facing and pursuing the enemy, and armies who charge, retreat, take up their position and throw themselves forward again. For three thousand years the tumult of battle, the gallop of cavalry and the trample of infantry echoed through the air. The Medes, the Persians, the Scythians and others all succeeded one another before the Iranian empire of Achaemenids was founded, first with Cyrus (559-

530 B.C.) and then the famous Darius (522-486 B.C.) and his successors. There was also the fall of Babylon, the glory of Persepolis and the fierce battles against the Greeks. In the 4th century B.C. the lightning raid of Alexander the Great of Macedonia as far as the Indus spelled the end of the Achaemenid dynasty.

Still in existence from this long period are harnesses found in the tombs of horsemen, bronze bridle bits for breaking in wild horses and decorative ornaments representing lancers in a flying gallop, as well as figurines of horse-drawn combat chariots and engravings on seals, on that of Darius for example; and, in the Scythian territory, notably at Pazyryk (in the Altaic region, USSR), in the 5th century B.C., funeral masks still fixed to the skeletons of horses, reproduced in cut felt, leather, gold and copper horsehair and a stags head with its antlers: a probable sign of Shamanist rites and the transfer of the solar symbol from the stag to the horse.

THE HORSE AND IMPERIAL SYMBOLISM

After the fall of the Achaemenids, one of Alexander the Great's lieutenants, Seleucus, settled in Iran

and founded the Seleucid Dynasty (3rd-2nd century B.C.), which maintained the Hellenistic culture. Here the horse did not apparently play any particular role although the sovereign continued to make his appearance mounted. Then, in 141 B.C., the Parthians seized the throne. This was a new dynasty, that of the Arsacids, who repulsed the attacks of Roman forces for two and a half centuries. Experienced horsemen, the Arsacids charged their assailants with a very mobile and effective light cavalry and used heavy cavalry to hold their positions. Their men were dressed in armour and helmet and their horses were protected by a long caparison made from leather plates fastened together with straps.

Their last king was killed in combat in 224 A.D. by the Iranian founder of the Sassanids (3rd-7th centuries A.D.) who took the empire to its peak of glory. The emperor was at the same time master and symbol of the empire. He was represented many times: on horseback, receiving the divine investiture, charging his enemies, fighting them in furious equestrian duels, or even remaining in the saddle in order to further the humiliation of his beaten enemies, who he sometimes trampled, in order to receive homage from his subjects and tribute from conquered peoples. One of these scenes depicts an event of special importance: sculptured on a vast rock

Following pages: The Boz-Kachi is one of the oldest equestrian games, as old as polo. Both originated on the high plateaux of Asia, and were practiced by those peoples who, even today, live with the horse according to their traditions. The Boz-Kachi is a battle for the possession of a decapitated sheep, whose skin must be brought to a determined point. Blows are allowed, but not dismounting to pick up the carcass.

On the left: A fragment of a mosaic found at Pompeii (2nd century B.C.) representing the clash between Alexander and Darius, during the decisive battle of Issos which opened the road to Alexander's conquest of Asia.

When the Muslim invasions submerged the Iranian empire and spread to Afghanistan and India, representations of the horse became closer to reality. There are many historical and scientific (above all veterinary) texts which were illustrated with precise drawings: equestrian battles, (like that opposite, a work of the Moghul school, late 16th century A.D.) or episodes of daily life (below: a mare suckling her, 17th century A.D., Museum of New Delhi.)

wall at Bishapur, it shows Shapur I accompanied by his horsemen, mounted in full glory on his horse, looking down on the Roman emperor, Valeria, kneeling as a sign of submission after the battle of Edessa (260 A.D.); thus is commemorated Iran's definitive victory over Rome.

Likewise the emperor hunted on horseback and numerous gilt silver plates show him galloping at full speed in the pursuit of abundant and various game.

Finally, the clearest proof that the horse was part of imperial symbolism is the throne on which the sovereign sat, in majesty, supported by two winged horses figured in profile. In this way, for example, he was represented at the centre of a famous gold cup, encrusted with jewels and rock crystal, from the 6th century, belonging to the treasure of Saint-Denis (now in the Medals collection of the National Library, Paris).

ARTILLERY WITH STIRRUPS

Towards 640-650 the declining Iranian empire surrendered to the first Moslem invasions. Throughout the centuries generation after generation of the peoples who converted to Islam surged into that part of Asia and spread largely towards the east, engulfing Afghanistan and almost the whole of India. Concurrently, the horse lost its sacred character. However, it conserved its privilege of being the mount of the king, important people within the kingdom, their guests, and the elite of the armies. Equestrian art was honored more than ever, just as the cavalry still played a leading part in territorial conquest.

The horse was linked with the ostentation of the court in its public displays, it was sought and acquired for sometimes exorbitant prices by monarchs and dignitaries, and it represented sumptuous presents, offered to them by their potential allies or given in homage to a brave warrior whom they recognized. It also participated in romance, since well-bred women knew how to ride as well as men, and there was no shortage of references to rides taken by lovers, either in literature, or in manuscript illustrations.

As the Moslem conquests over the Moghuls in India proceeded, from the 16th century onwards, the horse remained the mount of the emperor in his military undertakings, despite competition from the elephant during imperial hunts and certain festivals; for example the Maharajah of Hindu India

In Afghanistan, horses and costumes never change: an equestrian people finds it difficult to lose its identity.

72

Cavalry men and also civilian horsemen, pit themselves against one another in games of skill during popular gatherings. A millennial tradition, these gatherings permitted, up until the last few years, a common equestrian tradition for all classes of society and for people from different regions.

participated. At times, the Moghuls fought against local dynasties, such as the Rajputs and the Mahrattas maintaining the cavalry in the forefront of the army. From the 14th century until the second half of the 19th century, we even see leaders defending their territory at the head of their troops, riding hell for leather against their assailants. The introduction of artillery did not radically alter the way in which the horse was used in battle, since the mounted guns (in bronze) were pulled by a pair of beautiful and steady horses: this is what was called in the 17th century the artillery of the stirrups, which was always found in the entourage of the king, firing salutes for his arrival or his departure, and following

his every movement in hunts, military campaigns and travels, etc.

The era of the horse in these Indo-Iranian regions ended with World War Two. It is nonetheless necessary to point out that in India, at the end of the 20th century, a state cavalry still figures in the traditional march on national commemoration day, a parade composed mainly of modern arms and armoured vehicles.

73

THE HORSEMEN

OF ISLAM

Fortresses lost in the middle of the Syrian desert still bear witness to the battles fought over these sands. The paintings and mosaics which they hold perpetuate the lives of the equestrian peoples who built them.

The Middle East is a crossroads. The Western, Eastern and African worlds have always met on this ground and on its roads, privileged with commerce and blighted by wars of conquest. The horse, companion of the great invasions, crossed these regions many times. It even seems that its first appearance there was as a wild horse, during the great migrations which progressively led herds far from their cradle of origin, the high plateaux of Asia, in about 4000 B.C. The nomadic tribes were late to domesticate it, and a recent interpretation of Sumerian texts supports the thesis of its presence at man's side from the third millennium B.C.

In fact certain authorities assert that small domestic horses, very similar to the Asiatic type, participated in the nomadic life of the first shepherds. However, this role must soon have given way to what was to characterize the use of horses in these countries for many centuries: the harness was created, and the horse was from then on the motor of numerous army campaigns. The Persians, of course, but before them the Assyrians and the Egyptians, used chariots more than any other military body. When not in use for war, harnessing was used for hunting, as is witnessed in a great many bas-reliefs; but this is not to say that the horse was to remain restricted in that role. The strategic position of the Middle East, which was to be familiar with cavalry through the invasion of Alexander the Great in the 4th century B.C., and then much later, the Islamic wave which the Barbary and Arab horses were to help spread from the south towards the north as far as Constantinople. To this list must be added the Crusades, which introduced, for the first time into these regions, mounts of an origin other than the Mongolian species, from which stemmed the indigenous, and even African horses.

HOT AND COLD BLOOD

Nowadays, it is generally admitted that the large number of breeds of horse originated in the crossing of distinct species, which then evolved differently (according to the climate), after having migrated, into two distinct types of primitive horse: Mongolian, or Asiatic, called hot blooded and Nordic, called cold blooded.

This pottery figure dating from 2000 B.C., and kept in the Museum of Amman, seems to represent a small domestic horse close to the Asiatic type, and its creator has not omitted to represent the correct proportions.

Some authors have envisaged the presence in Central Africa of a third type, utterly different from the above-mentioned two (which are, in fact, quite similar). Nevertheless, recent works taking account of the absence of any trace dating before the introduction of offspring from the Asiatic type, squash this theory and confirm the general hypothesis.

The Crusaders brought with them their massive great horses, but in practice the influence of the introduction of Nordic blood is not apparent in the local breed. Also the Islamic requirements for purity in the breeding of the war-horses of Allah limited the cross-breeding between imported stallions and Arab mares. On the other hand, the West, seduced by the horses of the desert, imported them. This introduction of oriental blood was further enhanced by the arrival of the Arab cavalry, as far as Poitiers.

Thus the horse was, in the Middle East, the common factor between the different civilizations and ethnic groups who one after the other rose to power. Still, the horse no longer held the religious place which it had in the East, although vestiges of its supernatural provenance can be seen in such mythological creatures as the griffin.

At the same time it is necessary to put aside Egypt which, although geographically on the African continent, must be incorporated into the history of equestrian peoples of the Middle East. Its position, isolated from contact with its neighbors (because of the deserts to the East and West, and the Mediterranean sea to the north) facilitated the arrival of wild horses from the south, coming from the Sudan (then called Nubia). At that time, these animals could only have belonged to the famous third race, which is today disputed by scientists. It was therefore necessary to await the arrival of eastern horsemen or Egyptian expeditions to the east in order for domesticated horses to be introduced into that country.

THE HORSE OF EVIL

Thus, it would seem that a horse similar to that produced three thousand years later in South America, was introduced into Egypt from 1800 B.C. onward, but was not depicted (on the bas-reliefs, for example) for another two hundred years. For many years this time lag made people believe that the adoption of the horse by the Egyptians occurred at a later date but the absence of representation is explained by a taboo: it was prohibited to mention or depict the horse, sacred animal of Seth, God of Evil, and it was necessary to await the arrival of a new potent ethnic group for that restriction to end.

A bas-relief from the Palace of Amra, in Jordan, illustrating the hunting of wild horses; the mares and their foals were captured in order to make up domestic herds. Their importance was vital for the first nomadic peoples not only for their transport but also to provide them with milk and meat.

A curious parallel exists between this, and the Aztec belief in the arrival of warrior gods, with the landing of the Spanish and their horses. Besides, there remains almost nothing equestrian in the Egyptian relics of that period, while at the same time in Palestine a powerful equestrian civilization was developing. It was this people, the Hyksos, who from 1780 B.C., pushed by the massive migrations of the Hittites, established in Egypt their own supremacy and that of the horse. From that date the traces left by the horse multiply, Seth having become the supreme god and his sacred animal a symbol of power.

A number of skeletons discovered in or beside sarcophagi (at Deir-el-Bahari and Saqqarah, for example) prove that these horses were certainly of the Mongol type, but were already modified by climatic conditions and domestication, just like those rediscovered in Palestine or Syria. The head

Small horses descended from the herds of Central Asia allowed for new techniques in hunting and warfare, such as archery from horseback, represented here, or the charge with a lance. (Museum of Damas.)

On the right: A symbol of power, the horse remains the principal wealth of Sheik Soleiman Abu Fawzy of Azrak, even though the rifle has replaced traditional weapons, and the modern snaffle the ancient bridle bit.

is relatively strong and the back short, but the legs are slimmer, and become even more refined as time goes by. The silhouette lacks lightness when compared with today's oriental horses, and the size, not more than 1.45m, is more often than not about 1.25m. What is more, a wooden statuette dating from around 1400 B.C. shows a small stocky horse, whilst later representations portray a totally new agility, without doubt the result of intense selection in the breeding of military horses.

78

Egypt, was less isolated, due on the one hand to the ease with which the cavalry moved around, and on the other hand, to the accompanying development of a very important method of breeding in Nubia, from where military expeditions returned with the spoils of war. The local custom of burying horses allowed for the precise comparison of Nubian mounts with those of Egypt. The necropolis of the 10th century B.C. offers the spectacle of dozens of rows of graves in which lie the steeds of past kings. A tomb even more ancient and isolated, very high up the Nile, encloses an equestrian skeleton dating from 1400 B.C. which presents few morphologic differences from today's Barbary horse.

This supplementary reservoir of horses avoided the degeneration due to in-breeding, and from then on Egypt became an important supplier of mounts for the Roman Empire. Despite the vicissitudes of history, Egypt always maintained the reputation of her Arab horses, which are still prized today. In the state stud farms are found excellent mares, whose male offspring are sometimes offered as a present during royal or presidential visits. However, fillies, jealously guarded in order preserve the purity of the race, are rarely offered.

ARABIA, EYE OF THE ISLAMIC TYPHOON

Mecca and Islam are two names which evoke centuries of battles, holy wars and crusades. For us, they represent the true origin of the Arab horse. In 622 A.D., Mohammed had to leave his birthplace, where his religious ideas and the disciples he had gathered around him were very badly received. During his flight, and then in his triumphant return to Mecca, indigenous horses played a very important role. Descendants of the horses of the Asian plateaux, they were slender but hardy, virtually tireless. Mohammed immediately understood the advantage to be gained from the possession of a horse which was faster and more robust than the animals utilized by his adversaries (generally camels, much less manageable, or teams of mules); he insisted therefore, on using his influence over his followers, on the importance of the selected horse, and instituted a code of breeding.

Time does not seem to have touched this Petra shepherd, a face chiselled by the wind and the sun. Here is the spirit of the desert.

THE NUBIAN HORSE

This orientation towards a morphology better-adapted to their function (in this case warfare) illustrates well the passage of the horse from being a sacred animal to that of an indispensable tool, precious, but susceptible to the criteria of human choice. This selection, as well as being freer than in

These empirical measures very rapidly bore fruit: The best mares crossed with the fastest stallions frequently produced fine offspring, among which the fillies were carefully conserved as future brood mares. After the Koran, a breeder never had to part company with a mare. Still today, if custom demands that an Arab horse be offered to a distinguished guest, it is always a stallion.

The often difficult living conditions of Mohammed's disciples, who became soldiers of God, favoured that quality still more. Throughout the long expeditions in the semi-desert regions, horses and riders often shared allowances of dried fish, a few dates, and camel's milk. But Mohammed's encouragement of his followers to raise horses of a pure race (asil) had no religious quality attached to the animal. If these steeds had to be part of the family, it was as instruments for conquest and spreading the faith. The owner drew pride, not from the possession of a descendant of one of the Prophet's mares (of which tradition lists the ancestors of five distinct families, the most valued being those of the Choman and the Koheilan), but from their power to provide a superior instrument, a decisive trump card, in the battles of the Holy War.

A companion at all times, the horse still participates in the rhythm of the land. And if the materials used are a little more modern, tradition is respected: It is the women who complete the harvest.

This is how the Arab horse, hardened by the harsh climate of these regions, carried the Islamic fighters towards the north as far as Constantinople, and towards the west as far as the Atlantic. In every country that they crossed, they encountered easier living conditions than those in Arabia, cradle of the species, and many breeds became acclimatized in these regions, without the original type being modified. They remained small horses (1.40m to 1.55m to the withers), carrying a slender head with well dilated nostrils, lean legs and a generally grey coat. In the Middle East, this horse still remains the symbol of power and, now sedentary, each Emir possesses one or several stud farms. Every child of good family must know how to ride a horse and, if the riders no longer make war, glory can be acquired on the race course. A great stallion is still the pride of his trainer!

AROUND THE JORDAN, FROM SOLOMON TO LAWRENCE OF ARABIA

On the shores of Jordan, it seems that horsemanship was only practiced by the indigenous races after invaders arrived. The numerous kingdoms which existed there (Moabite, Ammonites, Nabataean) had important commercial activities, but their bas-reliefs and sculpture (kept in the archaeological museum of Amman) portray the horse solely as the mount of their successive conquerors. These invaders, the Assyrians, followed by the Persians, were great horsemen. The Hyksos, who had previously dominated the coastal areas, thanks to their cavalry had already secured Egypt. It is therefore not surprising to find, notably in the Old Testament, traces of a certain taboo in relation to the horse. Up until the period of Solomon, this sentiment seemed as strong as that which prevailed against dogs and pigs! Thus the patriarchs travelled on the back of an ass or camel, and a devoted Hebrew would never have mounted a horse. Perhaps this is what Saint John meant in the famous phrase of the Apocalypse: 'I looked and noticed a horse, and he who rode it was called Death'.

At the beginning of the Christian era, the horse was still rare in that region, and it was necessary to await the spread of the word of Islam in order for the desert tribes to use this steed more widely.

Meanwhile the horse, unlike the camel, was not able to live meagerly in the desert, and his breeding still remained dependent on a supply of fodder and grains which local cultures were not always qualified to produce. Moreover, raids became indispensable; otherwise, for the weaker and less fortunate breeders, the religious duty of keeping cavalry of quality meant there was less water to drink and less grazing land for the other animals (sheep, goats, camels). Breeding horses thus became, by force of nature, a symbol of warrior power and wealth.

The desert kingdoms were established thanks to the horse; thus the Caliphs of the Umaiyads dynasty, which controlled the whole region in the 7th and 8th centuries, built fortresses of sandstone, between which the nomadic Sheiks circulated in times of peace. Mushatta, Karameh, Azraq (a temporary command post of the famous Lawrence of Arabia during World War I) were successively strongholds, hunting posts, and lastly proof of the nomadic-peoples' efforts to try and keep a land which they loved, a world where their horses could gallop in peace. To visit them today is to experience the thrill of ancestral pastoral life. The bastions of resistance have hunting scenes in their courtyards (portrayed in frescoes so well preserved that you'd think they were painted yesterday), that are all made more real by the nearby sight of a few tents, beside which a rider, a hawk on his fist, readies himself for the ancient pleasure of the hunt.

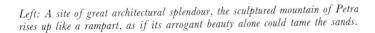

Left: A site of great architectural splendour, the sculptured mountain of Petra rises up like a rampart, as if its arrogant beauty alone could tame the sands.

Right: The mountain pass at Petra evokes memories of horsemen who have defended or attacked it throughout the centuries. And it is on horseback that the visitor appreciates its beauty.

Above: The Royal stud farm of Jordan possesses splendid pure-blooded Arab stallions. King Hussein himself, but mainly Princess Alia, directly supervise the running of the establishment. Despite the turbulent history of the country, pure breeds can be found here, and their forebears traced back precisely, in order to respect the obligations imposed by the W.A.H.O., the World Organization of the Arab Horse. Thus Jordanian horse breeding can now be considered as one of the finest in the Middle East. A green oasis, the Royal stud farm is a paradise for the horses.

Left: The Bedouins defend their individuality with success, at the heart of a world where nomadism is no longer really accepted. But their own culture, will and the richness of their history constitute a heritage which has become too important to lose. This is even more true in Jordan, whose recent past (from the beginning of the century) is made up of wars of liberation, in which the Bedouins were the first soldiers. Today, they still wear their costume in the same way as others wear a medal.

Right: From the summit of the temple of El Deir, in Petra, the view plunges down to the mountain passes which have seen so many cavalry gallop towards so many conquests.
But from all these dreams of glory, remain only the stones and equestrian traditions that the modern world has not yet obliterated.

STALLIONS OF THE DESERT

The traditional way of life still survives, despite challenges and vicissitudes, but the historical record of a nomadic people is, necessarily, sketchy. In the absence of great urban centres, libraries and archival material, cultural forms are the only record of a people's identity.

In geopolitical terms this region cannot be considered a nation until the end of World War I. The last official invaders, the Turks, considered it an Ottoman province until 1916. That year the Mohammedan sheriff Hussein ibn Ali, the Hashimite prince declared Emir of Mecca in 1908, proclaimed the independence of Hedjaz. Commanded by his son, the Emir Abdallah, the Arabian army, with mobile and determined cavalry, won numerous positions back from the retreating Turks. On July 5th, 1917, despite the fierce resistance of the German and Turkish armies, the port of Aqaba, on the Red Sea, fell to Arab troops led by Colonel Lawrence. The joining of forces of the English army and the Arab cavalry marked the end of a war, but not the definitive establishment of a new kingdom. The different aspirations of the combatants led to the disappearance of the Hedjaz. The Emir Abdallah, popular with many Bedouin tribes who occupied the region, founded the Transjordanian Emirate, which was granted independence from the British in 1923.

It was only in 1946 that the constitution established a hereditary monarchy, and the sovereign was crowned at Amman. When in 1952 the grandson of the worthy Emir Abdallah, first king of Transjordania, took over the throne of the country now called Jordan, he dutifully conserved the stable inherited from his grandfather, and a small number of horses from there formed the basis for a very strict breeding

Stallions are regularly worked without a saddle, or left free in order to develop and preserve their muscularity and vivacity. Heat is taken into account, and all exercise is taken early in the morning or at the end of the evening.

86

A view inside the Royal Stud of Amman: young Arab stallions at the horse-pond. Well cared for and relaxed, they maintain a truce while around the well. But if they find themselves in the presence of a mare, all their 'good education' is not enough to prevent them from fighting for the beauty. And the grooms carefully watch over the colts and fillies, in addition to each one remaining close by the young animal of which he is in charge.

policy which was then put into practice. The troubles undergone by the country, and the importance of by the horse, as much in the military field as the economic one, have led to unwise cross-breeding. In order to re-establish the pure race, King Hussein instituted severe controls for mating: the establishment of documents of origin and, for unregistered horses, recognition by the World Organization for the Arab Horse.

This program started with a dozen horses from the desert belonging to the Emir Abdallah and brood mares offered by the nomadic sheiks — always the workhorses and not those selected for racing. In this way the pure ancestral qualities of the asil horse were re-established: speed of course, but not to the detriment of robustness, affordability and all that made it the choice of Mohammed.

The royal stables today have more than a hundred horses, all of pure Arab race. They constitute a very

important centre for breeding. The young stallions, when they are not offered to a distinguished visitor, are sold throughout the entire world. As for the mares, they generally never leave the country, because of the traditional principles of conserving the asil lines, and the most beautiful make up the bulk of the brood mares in the stables. This policy of reproduction is supervised by a managing counsel over which the king himself presides! Horses remain an affair of state in the Middle East, even more so than oil.

THE MILLENNIUM OF THE HORSE

The African continent seems never to have had an indigenous wild equine population. The hypothesis that an equine species of its own evolved is no longer credited by scientists, due to the lack of any supporting paleontological evidence. As for theories about a more or less belated arrival of migrant herds from the plateaux of Central Asia or Europe, their credibility is greatly diminished by the natural barriers of the Red Sea and the deserts in the East, as well as that of the Mediterranean Sea in the north. It is therefore reasonable to attribute the introduction of the horse to the African continent to man, through his conquests and by horse breeding. An examination of the Tassili rock drawings lends credence to this interpretation.

vehicle consisting of a light platform on wheels. At the same time, the creators of these rock designs, without doubt Aegean, are very likely to have brought their mounts into this territory on their arrival. This would support the theory of the absence of the horse in relation to man in North Africa; but, the unique technique of harnessing employed strongly suggests an indigenous evolution.

A recent experimental study, using a reconstituted model of the depicted harness and vehicle, shows these horsemen, not as inheritors of a previous equestrian tradition, but as creators of a totally new and practical solution to the problem posed by animal

THE HARNESSING OF THE GREEN SAHARA

In the central Sahara, notably at Tassili in Ajjer (specifically at Tamadjert's cave), there are a number of outline drawings of harnessed horses. Generally Neolithic in date, Bronze Age, or a little later, these drawings are among the oldest of their type. They prove beyond doubt the presence of an already advanced, domesticated horse, used for drawing a

Punic piece illustrating a hunt scene, the light cavalry, the strength of Carthage. Helmet, lance and small round shield resemble Roman arms, 'fellow enemies' of the Carthaginians.

Left: A green valley among desolate rocks and a village which blends into the side of the spur overlooking the river.

traction: the problem of how to harness draught horses. The most universally accepted solution to this question (taking account of the load pulled, as well as the endurance and speed of the puller), are traction by the chest (as with Greek chariots and modern chest harnessing) or traction by the shoulders (as with Egyptian chariots and horse collar). The well preserved details of numerous cave drawings depict a frontal form of traction, the harness strap and support being fixed to a head harness which is made up of a halter without a forehead strap. The entire weight, as well as the force, is then applied, as is explained by J. Spruyette in his essays (Experimental Studies in Harnessing), on the throat lash of the bridle, but in no way restricts the throat, and therefore the respiration, of the horse. Under these conditions, a light wooden platform tied, in accordance with the technology of the time and the rediscovered drawings, can be pulled for quite a long time at a good pace, and is just as easy to handle whilst hunting as it is in combat. Unfortunately, insufficient evidence prevents a precise description of this civilization, which seems to have regressed rapidly with the dessication of the region. This method of harnessing was lost, and we have to wait for the Roman Conquest in order to rediscover in this area any mention of riders or equestrian technique.

FROM WHITE KNIGHTS TO BLACK RIDERS

The new introduction of Western horses probably dates the development of the Barbary horse in North Africa. Tough, temperate and courageous, it is bigger than the Arab horse and appears more rustic. The Carthaginian cavalry made it a noted mount from early times and it was quickly adopted by the Romans, the eternal enemies of Carthage. It was they who brought back Punic horses to Europe, in order to improve the breed of their Northern ancestors. Some of these horses were involved in the Gallic Wars, and were crossed with much bigger horses (the heavy draught horse from the Boulogne region or the Ardenne), which gave a certain agility to the offspring thus produced.

Even so we still have to ascertain the influence of the environment on the development of the horse, and the Barbary horse is only really comfortable in its ideal environment on the southern shores of the Mediterranean. The harsh climate (very hot days and freezing nights), the meager food and difficult terrain, make for a hardy animal, with a close rapport with man. It is in this way that the Barbary horse participated the history of the Garamantes people who for a long time were considered mythical. Inheritors of Western equestrian traditions, these Europeans, driven from the shores of the Mediterranean by the Carthaginians, plunged deep into

How many triumphant cavalry have passed under this arch in Algeria? It is today the only remains of great cities built by the Carthaginians and Romans on the coast of North Africa.

أنهى إليه نزك عن فرسه وبجدله وحماه وطاطأ رأسه فقال له أكبار وزماحباً

ثم جك ري ا عزل فلما مع المك بجعة وم برسنج حرسه ربه وسوى

كلد إيها الملك ومالي أري المغنتمرا ولاأري بجك عليك ولا أكليك على ياسك قناه

Towards the northeast and the west, the Islamic wave swept all other cultures away and increased the integration which commerce had already established between the Mediterranean shores and the Asiatic plateaux. (Rabat Library.)

the heart of the African continent where they imposed their military supremacy until the 10th century A.D. armed like the horsemen of ancient times, in a coat of mail and a leather and steel helmet (plate armour was still not invented), with sword and lance wedged in the saddle bow. They were only defeated by the greater numbers of Almoravids who, from Morocco, surged as much towards the east and south as to the north and to Spain.

In black Africa, the Almoravids were soon usurped by other Moslems, the Hausas, who bolstered their numbers with horsemen of the Garamantes. However, these black Moslems were not to rule for very long, and other horsemen gathered behind their Commander of the Faith, and came in their turn to dominate this region, which is the Cameroon of today.

Without doubt the descendants of these Westerners, driven from North Africa first by the Romans, then by the Arabs and the Peuls (also called Fulahs) were just simple nomads who, driving their herds before them, were subjected to successive overlords without integrating with them (although a number of racial cross-breeds must have resulted, above all with the Garamantes), but partaking of the economic, political and military benefits. So when one of their own people, Ousman Dan Folio, an intelligent and impassioned prophet, rose up and declared a holy war, only a few months were needed for them to form a swift and maneuverable mounted army. This Peul cavalry demolished the armored Hausa troops and integrated them into their own forces! This policy bore fruit on the battlefield in the new kingdom, and still today, in the great Fulah gatherings, it is the Hausas who parade in armour, lance in hand and sword at their side. However, given the heat, we might think that the Hausa armour is a rather malicious requirement on the part of the Peul rulers.

91

Often represented on popular paintings, the game of canes is one of the most ancient Ethiopian contests, clearly demonstrating the methods of combat practiced by these Africans at the beginning of their equestrian career.

Right: Also on the Niger, the horse is present at all great occasions, as here at the enthroning of the Sultan of Zinder and Damagaram

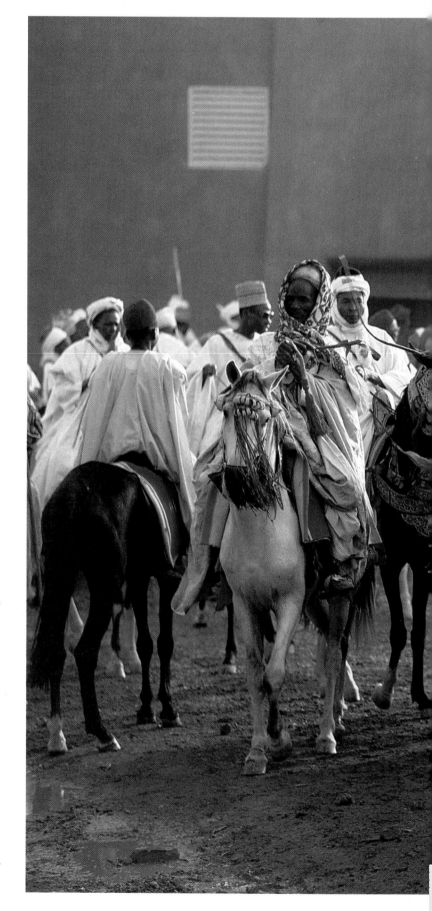

ONCE AN EQUINE PARADISE: ETHIOPIA

Nubia, to the south of Egypt, was a later but important source of horses. We have seen that the first dynasties of the Pharaohs did not have the benefit of equestrian knowledge, due to the absence of horses, but that those horses which were introduced by the Hyksos into Egypt formed a real bond between the Middle East and Africa. This role is very important, since it seems that the equine species was not developed on the African continent, and after their acclimatization in Egypt, it was by way of penetration down the Nile that they spread to the more southerly regions. In fact, Egyptian texts from around 1360 B.C. describe the capture and destruction of more than 300 stallions by a military expedition to Nubia. The discoveries of numerous remains of horses in the tumuli of their deceased masters confirm the relationship of these small horses (1.20 m to 1.8 m to the withers) to those of Egypt in the same period. The strong head, the short

92

back and the general lack of delicacy tend to show inferior breeding techniques, which were to produce better results at a later date.

Yet this region was the birthplace of the horses whose descendants, crossed without doubt with Arabian horses, which were imported across the Red Sea or the Gulf of Aden — at that time great trade routes — were going to populate southern Sudan and the Ethiopia of today. In these regions of high plateaux, horses were to find favorable conditions for their development. Whilst the culture of the region was largely Arabic, it was nonetheless open to Western influences. The horses, well adapted to the climate, gave rise to intense commercial activity, and were exported to Central Africa and to the south. Despite all this, the Ethiopian region, a para-

dise for horses, remained for a very long time, and it was here that there existed for many centuries a supply of semi-wild horses, whose number surpassed three million at their peak. Sadly, the recent disastrous droughts, whilst reducing the country and its inhabitants by famine, has simultaneously caused a collapse of horse breeding and the hope of an early return to prosperity which it represents. Nowadays the decline of the horse is still from time to time a symptom of social catastrophe for a still rural civilization, in the same way as it was in the times of the first horsemen. And even outside support of the economy, if it does not restore this tradition of equine importance, can only mark the end of a thousand-year-old culture.

THE WAR HORSE OF THE DJEBEL

Morocco presents, to the eyes of amateur historians, the considerable advantage of being geographically on the edge of a world, and thanks to horses and the cultures which they have helped to establish, this country is, for any rider, a dream come true. From the 2nd century B.C., the Berbers, inhabitants of these regions, offered the Roman conquerors the use of a Barbary horse of Carthaginian origin; and this horse was such a fountain of strength that they managed to transform, for the first time (but not for the last) the foothills of the Atlas into impregnable fortresses. The high rocky plateaux seamed by green valleys, all protected by passes and ravines, formed natural defenses and thus became the Berbers' traditional refuge, from where their robust horses allowed them to descend upon and take enemy columns by surprise. It is in this way that they also held themselves outside the range of the Arab wave which arrived, in the 8th century A.D., on the Atlantic shores, 'there, where the sun no longer sets on the earth'.

After their victorious resistance to several Arab dynasties, the Berbers, converted to Islam, founded their own dynasties, notably those of Almoravids and Almohads. The importance of the horse was then overriding, and the importance of horse breeding justified the Koranic laws introduced by the Moslem religion. The supremacy of their mounts,

As this travel poster advertised it at the beginning of the century in Morocco, the arrival of the sovereign in each one of the holy towns is an occasion for great equestrian festivities.

besides giving the warriors of the Rif (the Western part of the Middle Atlas) the chance of installing one of their own on the throne, later on (in the next century), created enormous problems for the European colonizers, since modern military techniques proved inadequate to keep in check the spirit of the mountain riders. What is more, the French army recognised the value of these riders and integrated into its cavalry corps native soldiers and mounts who performed marvels on many occasions. They could still be seen marching on the Champs-Elysées in Paris, years later.

Having modernized, Morocco did not absolutely deny the horse the place which it had held throughout its history and the importance of the cavalry and the royal stables remain as proof of this. However, mechanization and certain climatic catastrophes have forced horse breeders to find a solution to the unsuitability of the two principal breeds to modern economic conditions. Cross breeding of the two oldest African horses has resulted in the Arab-Barbary horse, which blends satisfactorily the robustness of the Carthaginian horse with the high spirits of the mounts of Islam. Today it is undoubtedly in this new breed, which may have been established many centuries ago but which tradition rejected, that the continued value of the North African horse at the side of man is found.

We know that drought has ravaged this continent for many years and that even the most northerly countries (Morocco, but also Algeria and Tunisia) have seen their pastures dried by the sun, earlier

In the Atlas, a marriageable girl does not remove her veil; but a Berber would say: 'In the eyes of a girl, like in those of a horse, you can read all her qualities.'

Left: the everyday mount, the donkey, is the unappreciated cousin of the horse.

each year. Horses are valued but are considered to be symbols of family wealth, and are the first to be affected in times of shortage, when cattle and sheep, sources of food, take priority with regard to the distribution of grain and forage. The Arab horse, capable of the utmost affordability when it accompanies its Bedouin master in the desert, is here more sedentary and must accomplish very energetic tasks in order to travel the path for which it is intended. With the shortage of grain, the national stud farms, accompanied by a few large private breeders, are the only establishments able to maintain the horse. As for the Barbary, so far inseparable

97

from life in the mountains or the Berber valleys, it now reveals itself, because of these difficult conditions, to be less strong and more gluttonous than the ox; and thus is disappearing from agricultural undertakings, and even from the dumb animal transport market, where it is being replaced by the ass and the camel.

RECOGNITION OF THE BASTARD

In this land, where the two breeds, traditionally considered as very different, seemed destined to vanish from daily life, a third, uniting the qualities of the first two, may win favour with the populace. This question has for many years been the subject of a wager taken up by Moroccan stud farms. The Arabian-Barbary, which existed shamefaced because of the cohabitation of the two races, can finally see its individuality recognised and appreciated. When the warriors of Islam pushed their Arab

Above: On the high plateaux of the Atlas mountains, only the Barbary horses — or the Arab-Barbary bastards — can stand up to the hard conditions of life.

Previous pages: The high point of the festival in the majority of Islamic countries, is without doubt the reliving of the memory of their irresistible conquering charges.

mounts as far as the Atlantic shore, it was unthinkable for them to accept cross-breeding of their brood mares of pure race with the more primitive mounts of those taking refuge in the mountains. In the end contact was peacefully re-established, exchanges were instigated and before long an osmosis occurred between the two ethnic groups, the result of the union between their horses. However, the Islamic religion considers the purity of the Prophet's mares to be so important that hybrid foals were still considered as bastards unworthy of reproducing or even of being mounted by honorable riders.

It took, therefore, an ecological catastrophe, along with mechanization, to give the Arab-Barbary

100

In a country with stony soil, horseshoeing is an art which developed alongside that of horsemanship. Right: the necessary equipment (minus the nails) to shoe a horse for one year.

Below: Fillies let loose at the Meknes stud farm, situated in ancient fortifications, near a park of several hectares.

its chance. A good cross-bred horse inherited the relatively large size (1.60m to the withers) and the robustness of its Barbary relatives, and the pride and harmony in the silhouette of the fiery Arab horse. Solid and rustic, it continued to be able to live and travel the mountains of meager pastures and rocky slopes, but it also had the necessary gentleness and courage for all the current sporting disciplines: jumping obstacles, dressage and endurance. With good limbs, dry (without fat) muscles, and the pleasing appearance of a lively but comfortable mount, this horse suited perfectly both the new demands of these regions and those of the classic horse clubs.

Currently, the national Moroccan stud farms supply private breeders, beleaguered by the drought. All mares brought there by their owners are bred to the national stallions, and provided that the offspring is afterwards identified and 'recognised' as belonging to the correct mare after birth, it is entered into the regularly organized races for young horses. This is how this breed, whose beautiful offspring were reserved as official blood stock, was developed: thus two Arab-Barbary stallions live side by side with cousins of pure race in the stables of Meknes. Numerous national mares are foaled with foals of that race, the choicest of which remain in the stables, where they will put their genetic qualities to the service of horse breeders from other parts of the country. And the demand is growing: the royal cavalry, equestrian centres and individual riders for sport or leisure, these are the new users of this made-to-measure horse!

Of course tradition remains strong, and from the classic horse shows, emerge great scenes of cavalry combat, with charges enacted at full gallop and the firing of muskets; the Arabs are always going to mount their little grey horses, more or less direct descendants of the companions of the conquerors of the 8th century. Moreover, the Berber will parade more willingly to the moussem on a robust horse with a chestnut coat, or a bay horse; and if this beautiful Barbary horse were no longer to exist, then without doubt he would come on foot. But generally this change is well received, and seems to be the best thing for the continued survival of horses in the country: it ensures their preservation in the daily life of the people.

THE ARISTOCRATIC

HORSE

The spirit, elegance and pride of the horse have marked western history more materially than in Asia or the Middle East: it has been a symbol of power, then a sign of nobility; and later as a pulling force synonymous with making work easier. But, free, it is always so beautiful!

Let's take a look at Europe, from the Urals to the Atlantic and at islands large or small, near or far. Of course in Europe we find mountains and plateaux: the Alps, the Bihor in Rumania, the highlands of Scotland, the Massif Central, the Carpathians and the Pyrenees, the barrier separating the mainland and the Iberian peninsula. However we very quickly see that, for the most part, Europe is made up of plains and steppes, areas ideal for the proliferation and development of horses. Throughout the ages, horses have multiplied and become widespread here without difficulty. For even if it is hard for us 'civilized' people to accept this idea, up until the last century, frontiers, administrative barriers and customs were almost nonexistent, or could be bypassed. Fences and barbed wire were yet to be invented. And through the centuries, indeed through millenniums, right up until very recently, horses freely or through necessity (climatic changes, predatory action, etc.) wandered around and across the continent settling here and there in regions which were destined to become the cradles of particular breeds.

The European breeds of horse are the most numerous and the most diverse. They have often been, and still are, influenced by man and the selection which he makes between one or another in accordance with his needs. The history of the horse and horsemen in the Old World is a long one, so let's start in the extreme East, with the country of the Cossacks.

THE COSSACKS: RIDERS FROM THE CRADLE

The Cossacks are a curious people who, from before the year 1000, established their communities between the Sea of Azov and the Caspian, along the shores of the Don, the Kuban and the Terek and on the first foothills of the Urals. They were made up of outlaws, fugitives, bandits and rebels who, avid for great horizons and adventure had continuously sought refuge in the Free Country. Some found adventure living on boats and for a long time Cossacks plundered the rivers and shores of the Black Sea, but in the end these uncouth men were to find adventure on the backs of their horses, animals which could devour space. Very quickly the Cossack communities were to form one of the most formidable cavalries in the world. It remained so up until the end of the Second World War.

The first word a Cossack child was taught to say was 'horse'. The horse with whom he was required to live made for an unusual way of life. The horse of the steppe, energetic and even-tempered, possessed hardly any panache, but did have extraordinary strength and endurance. As soon as a child could stand, or even before, he learnt how to ride, and very quickly he could cover considerable distances in the saddle, and work out such distances according to how tired his horse was. He was also very quickly initiated into those actions on horseback which were indispensable to life on the steppe, and soon became

The history of horses and horsemen on the 'old continent' is long. Notable proof of this is the engravings on the funeral stelae which confirm the social importance of the horse. (Budapest)

What is known of the Cossacks is illustrated quite well by this engraving illustrating the book Tarass Bulba: *which shows their clothing (the famous astrakhan hat), cavalry equipment (spurs, saddle with stirrups), weapons (lance and lasso) and their equestrian skill.*

a warrior. The young Cossack, went from walking to riding to galloping in no time. He then would learn how to stand in his saddle while galloping, so that he could scan the unending plains as far as possible. Mimicking the appearance of a dead rider who takes his feet out of his stirrups, or hangs, still galloping, under the belly of his horse were two movements designed to fool the enemy and take him

by surprise. When he had become a fine horseman, and when he had become accustomed to using arms such as the saber and lance, then the musket and later on the rifle, he had become a true cossack. He was now ready to join the sotnia, the village squadron, led by the ataman, the elected leader.

The call to war unleashed the almost instantaneous mobilization of the sotnias from different voskois (clans) which formed armies of professional warriors and cavalry for whom battle was life itself. Throughout the centuries, such expeditions were frequent and absences were often very long. Sometimes it was a question of going to pillage such and such a rich city in order to stock up on supplies — the Cossacks refused to cultivate the land and bred few of their horses. Sometimes it was a matter of support for an ally or a fight for a generous share of the plunder. On horseback, the Cossack felt strong enough to go to the end of the world, and there he went.

FROM THE PACIFIC TO THE CHAMPS-ELYSEES

It is impossible to recount here in detail the epic story of the few hundred Cossacks who, in the 16th century, snatched Siberia from the Tartars. In ten years, their long venture led them past the shores of the Don and Kuban to those of the Pacific! It also brought about the transformation of their outlawed state to that of elite cavalry of the Muscovite Empire, and this simply by offering the Czar Ivan IV the territories which they had just conquered. It was however a turbulent alliance which the Czar had made! For, free, but as credulous as they were naive, the Cossacks, for a long time to come, dreamt only of riding at the head of a raid or into battle. Any battle, or almost!

Bogdan and Mazzepa were among the 'atamans' who led the horsemen of the steppe into battle against the Poles, Swedes and even the Russians. Peter the Great was fond of them and while paying a visit to their country of the Don, decided upon their emblem: a naked but armed Cossack, spinning on horseback!

Uprisings, rebellions, battles and wars followed,

During a certain frosty period in their relations with Imperial Russia, the Cossacks were caricatured as formidable eaters of raw meat (that of their enemies?).

Left: Hungarians of the Putza in traditional costume.

until in 1799, the Cossacks found themselves facing the French army in Italy, at Bergamo. Without waiting for the Russian engineers to finish their work, Platov, who commanded them, gave the order to cross the river by swimming with their horses: a very common exercise for the Cossack! And, for the first time, the French saw sweeping down on their battalions, these bearded cavalry, dressed in leather and fur, wearing fur hats, and riding strange little horses harnessed with wooden saddles covered with sheepskin shabracks. It was the first time, but not the last: Marengo, Friedland and Austerlitz followed.

107

The Cossacks were a formidable presence in the Russian ranks, to such an extent that at the Tilsit summit, Napoleon asked the Czar to present their leader, Platov.

In 1812 the Grande Armée surged into Russia, observed very closely by Cossack detachments who knew the terrain and knew how to, if necessary, conceal their horses by making them lie down. Moscow was burning. The Grande Armée made an about-face, but was overwhelmed by the cold and snow and harassed by the Cossack sotnias. Very quickly, combat between the French cavalry and that of Platov became rare: the horses of the Hussars and dragoons of the Emperor were less hardy than those of the steppe and stood up badly to the rigors of the climate and the lack of food (very few made it back to France), whilst the nasty, little badly harnessed horses of the Cossacks, used to the terrain and Russian winter, maintained their vivacity and endurance and made their riders into active wasps, attacking the flanks of the disintegrating French army.

One dark night, during a campaign near Troyes in Champagne, Napoleon himself was only a whisper away from being captured by a detachment of Cossacks. It was the Cossacks who were the first to penetrate defeated Paris, filing past the Czar and installing their horses and bivouacs among the cafes of the Champs-Elysées!

ONLY A PROVERB REMAINS

Throughout the 19th century, the Cossacks, organized in a regular army, with uniforms, regiments and rules, fought valiantly for the Czar against the Chinese, Japanese, English and Turks. From 1870, they also became what the revolutionaries called the valets of the regime, in charge of repressing public uprisings and demonstrations. The sotnias of free horsemen had become instruments of oppression and had, in a way, lost their soul.

In 1917 the Czar fell and the Cossacks went from the frying pan into the fire. The revolution and its issues were beyond them. The social order, which had been overturned by the new masters of Russia, no longer made sense to them. War and horses remained, but they no longer fitted in with that taste for personal freedom which had made their ancestors lovers of the steppe, the wind and the stars.

In 1945 an S.S. General, Von Pannwitz, succeeded in reassembling the Cossacks for the last time. They elected him their general 'ataman' and, under his orders once more rode into battle, with their famous cry, 'Huzzah!' They charged with swords drawn, they seized batteries of artillery, and although they knew how to swim across rivers, they used modern equipment, rubber dinghies, to cross the water on horseback.

The escapade was brief. The Great War came to an end, the Reich collapsed and Von Pannwitz was forced to surrender to the English, who sent the Cossacks back behind the future Iron curtain, but kept their horses. It was a symbolic separation. For the Cossacks it was the end. Hardly anything remained of the proud riders of the steppe, save the proverb of the Don: 'When the Cossack is on horseback, only God is greater than he'.

CURIOUS BREEDS AND CROSS-BREEDS

The Cossack is no more, nor is his horse that once galloped across endless plains. Nothing remains of him. For if a few horses of the Don still exist, they are no longer worth consideration since the ugly little horses, children of the steppe, have been crossed with oriental breeds and then with thoroughbred horses. Improved, they have increased in size and in power, but it is doubtful if they will ever be superior to their ancestors in strength and endurance.

Karabakh, Karadin, Lokai and Kustanair are only some of the breeds raised today in the USSR, and many have been carefully selected in the state stables. However, the most famous of these breeds are without question the Orlov and the Akhal-Teke.

The Orlov, or Russian trotter, is powerful, of good size, and an excellent stepper. Apt to be nimble and suited to the saddle, it has more endurance than true speed, and its courage and energy make it a very popular horse. All the Orlovs descend from the same stallion, Bars I, born around 1800 in the

With his leather boots, his wide trousers and the handle of his whip hanging at his side, the guardian of the herd on the Hungarian plains is internationally recognizable.

racing horse that exists. Apart from the races themselves and a few minutes at the end of the day, seven blankets are left on its back continually. Its diet is based on, among other things, barley mixed with eggs and butter. The weaknesses of the golden horse are its stubborn character and its ungainly way of jumping.

However, this horse may do more for detente than computers. For example, in the USSR, every effort has been made over the past thirty-odd years to establish a new breed by crossing the Metis with the Orlov and the American standard bred trotter!

RIDERS OF THE PUSZTA

Without worrying ourselves with frontiers, or visas for that matter, let us make a jump westward, over the Carpathians, in order to reach the Hungarian Puszta. Here again we find a flat country under an enormous sky and a plain fit for raising horses and undertaking long rides.

The Puszta is a plain set apart from the contamination of civilization, on which herds of grey longhorn cattle and beautiful fleecy Ratzka sheep graze side by side with horses. The people who live here, the Csikos, settled on this land more than ten centuries ago, and they have since resisted all movement of history. For them nature remains almost intact, and horses and livestock are of the highest importance.

stud farm of Count Orlov. Currently, some 35,000 stock are registered.

There is no doubt that its golden coat with silver flecks (a coat which can also be grey and sometimes bay) has made the reputation of the Akhal-Teke. Originating from the Asian plateaux, this strange horse, which some regard as the Arab's ancestor, has many other special features. With its long svelte body, its slender head and expressive look, it is a gracious and swift saddle-horse. It enjoys dressage and can be an excellent jumper. Furthermore, it is surely the most unusually trained and cared for

FROM NOMADS TO HUSSARS

It was at the beginning of the 9th century that the Magyar tribes, who some say descended from the Huns of Attila, pursued and driven from the steppes by more warlike and powerful peoples, made the immense plain of the Danube and the Tisza their own. Having always been nomads, the Magyars settled there, but continued to devote themselves to the only activity of which they felt truly capable (and for which the country was ideal), that of rearing horses.

Two centuries later, the peaceful kingdom of the

Magyar was overturned by the invasion of the hordes of Genghis Khan, and their country, like so many others, was crushed and overrun. This was only the beginning of almost uninterrupted upheaval, which, for better or worse, but often for worse, they were going to have to come to terms with.

Turks, Poles, Russians, Austrians and others turned the Puszta into an almost permanent battle field. Colonized by one army, annexed by another, it was a pantry from which one could feast shamelessly and also, perhaps above all, a formidable reservoir for the remounting of cavalry. What was valued

most were its horses, hardened by the winds and the abrupt changes in temperature.

There were one hundred and fifty years of Turkish domination, and division of the country between Turkey and Austria, before the latter secured the whole area. However, the Hungarians were not sub-missive and uprisings were frequent. First of all, they developed cavalry techniques for combat, and bold charges to fight the enemy and simply to survive. And it was this necessity to survive that gave rise to the legendary Betyars, beloved bandits who extorted riches from the well-off to redistribute them to the poor. All their strength lay in the speed andendurance of their horses.

As horsemen, the Hungarians were imitated throughout Europe. The Hussar, a light cavalry soldier, for a long time indispensable to any army, was only a more or less retouched copy of the Hungarian Huszar, who was just as able and fast. On the shores of the Danube, his shako was called

Certain equestrian feats are specific to the Csikos, such as driving five horses, three in front and standing on two behind. And the feathered hat, the ample shirt and the embroidered waistcoat are a must

a 'csako' and his dolmen (the jacket which was worn hung from the shoulder) was a 'dolmany'. As for the golden Brandenburgs which he bore on his chest, they are still found today on the dress jackets of some Csikos who, at the end of the 20th century, are still riders of the great plain, just like their ancestors.

A STRANGE SILHOUETTE

The Csiko spends the greater part of his existence in the company of his horse. With it he guards his herds, separates them, moves and looks after them. But also, together, they travel and scour the Puszta

In work clothes: hat, waistcoat, full trousers and boots, whip at the side and saddle on the shoulder.

which is open and hardly marked by roads or fences. This way of life makes the horse and man partners. The animal learns his work and his trade and the rider learns to teach his mount. What a spirit and feeling for the horse! In order to judge him, you only have to observe the degree to which the Csiko can control the training of his mount. The horse of the Csiko lies down on command, mounted or not, and does it perfectly; whilst stretched to his full length, neck, withers and head on the ground, it allows its rider to stand upright on its shoulders! It also knows how to sit, a little bit like the way a dog does, and shows neither discomfort nor surprise when its rider climbs up onto its hindquarters.

As well as a teacher, the Csiko is also a master, and the harmony that reigns in the five-in-hand teams of horses which he brings together never fails to amaze. Teams of horses which draw vehicles can also be used without drawing anything at all. Holding the reins of five horses — two behind and three in front —, the Csiko stands on the two behind, one foot on each hindquarter, then makes the five animals perform maneuvers at the gallop!

The silhouette of the Csiko, or the poulinier, to use the French term, is formed from his fawn-coloured boots over which spill his voluminous trousers, reminiscent of a skirt; the sleeves of his shirt, which emerge from a black felt waistcoat, and are as ample as those of a ball gown; and his small round hat with its turned-up edge which is reminiscent of ancient Chinese hair styles. But when in the saddle, galloping, his clothes puffed out by the wind, in total unity with his horse and the infinity of the Puszta, he is *the* rider, powerful and free, the likes of which are now almost unknown in Europe.

BLACK BULLS AND WHITE HORSES

Let's return to the map of Europe. In Hungary, and also in Poland, we have seen that the horse, mounted and harnessed, has always had a place in the daily routine. However, as we push further towards the West — Germany, Austria, and France, towards the highly industrialized countries, this is no longer the case. Here the horse has disappeared from the roads and streets, and horse-drawn vehicles and riders

The herdsmen always gather herds of horses on horseback, for the Camargue horses live in semi-freedom in the Rhone delta.

Following pages: At sunset, in the marshes, the free animals pass by as pleasing shadows; and the little horses do not fear the meeting with the black bulls, who are equally at home in this place. There is no enmity between them in the wild.

have been usurped by automobiles. Yet, although less visible than before, the horse is far from having disappeared. Conservatories, such as the Vienna School and its Lippizaner horses, or the Cadre Noir of Saumur (French Army School of Horsemanship), maintain the equestrian tradition, and everywhere to some extent, the civilization of leisure has transformed the ancient companion of work into that of games and relaxation. Civilization has sanctioned, and will always do so, the preservation and development of the equine species in danger of extinction. Furthermore, scrutinizing the map a little more closely, we discover a minuscule area, in the south of France, where horse and man still live in harmony: the Camargue.

The Camargue with its mysterious marshlands is the domain of the black bull and the white horse. No one knows where they came from. The only certitude is that they have lived there since time immemorial, and bulls from the Camargue have a strange resemblance to those depicted on the walls of caves by prehistoric men.

In his time, Julius Caesar became aware of the value and the qualities of the Camargue horse and in order to replenish the Roman cavalry, it is said that he had two stud farms built, one at Arles and the other at Rhodensia. What are the qualities of the horse from the marshlands?

First, a surprising rusticity and endurance; next, an aptitude to come to terms with mud and sand, in other words, agility; and last, a willing character,

Tradition is found in a cross-breed of the Arlesian and the Camargue horse, which evokes the music of the Midi.

of a kind rarely found. Its only fault, if you can call it that, is its modest size (from 1.35m to 1.45m). It is in order to compensate for this small size, while conserving its other qualities, that man is constantly straining his ingenuity to cross it with taller and more powerful animals. However all has been in vain, and not one attempt has had a lasting effect on the breed. Life in this cradle, this very special habitat of the delta of the Rhône, eliminates one by one all of the foreign genetic traits.

From the Middle Ages until the beginning of this century, one month a year was allocated to the treading out of grain, real drudgery which consisted of circling each day 80 to 90 kilometers in round circles in grass which came to knee level. None of the breed which were sometimes substituted in the

Camargue to carry out this task could keep to the necessary rhythm!

Sultan is the name of a mount which belonged to the Baron of Baroncelli, who around 1910, established a record which is still famous. In four days, the horse and its rider covered the 450 kilometers separating Saintes-Maries-de-la-Mer from Lyon in only forty-three hours of actual riding.

Furthermore, the priceless white horse is totally at ease with the black bull. It is born and grows up in its company, in freedom. This close contact between the two is found across the marshlands and stretches of samphire. The horse learns early on to understand all the bull's habits and reactions, which makes it an indispensable helper for the keeper of the bulls in his traditional work.

DANGEROUS YET JOYFUL GAMES

It has to be for the famous provincial games that the keeper still exists. The festivals, which pay homage to the bull, might have originated from Crete where the cult of the bull was born, and where the bull was often the emblem of the sun for ancient peoples. In the Delta region, hundreds of games take place each year, between April and September. There are games for which bulls are necessary, and the keepers and their horses guard and take care of the five hundred or so herds, totalling almost 15,000 head.

A good half of the keeper's life is spent in the saddle. He must ridge the marshlands, on ground sometimes muddy and slippery and at other times cracked by the heat of the sun, in order to control the position and the condition of the animals, to stop them escaping, from the space to which they are assigned or in order to move them. When the time comes, it is he who has the job of conveying the competition bulls from one village to another, from one arena to another, and from one festival to another.

In springtime the ferrade takes place, the branding of the young bullocks (the anoubles), a ceremony to which all the keepers of the herd are invited. On horseback, the keepers assemble the animals and, one by one, the anoubles are picked out. This involves grabbing them by the horns and making them lie down. Those on foot chase the bulls who in turn charge them, and in addition riders intrepidly throw themselves from the height of their saddle on to the head of the formidable animal with the black coat, while riding at full speed!

The equestrian games, such as the bouquet game,

The games of the Camargue are varied, but centre on two indispensable features in the daily life of the region: the horse, and the bull, which is smaller and less dangerous than in Spain. Some prefer to symbolise it with rosettes on a carved head.

are as much a chance for the keeper to demonstrate his riding ability as the skill of his mount. But it is in the abrivado which he gives his all. The abrivado consists of leading the bulls from their pasture to the arenas, often some distance away. Reunited as a team who know each other well and possess a precise technique, the keepers, after having rounded them up, surround four, five or six bulls in a vertible wall of horse flesh and lead them along the sheep tracks towards the village and the arena. The bulls, who are excitable, often gallop! The work is, at the very least, rough, as much for the horses as for the riders. It becomes even more so when the local people and visitors, as tradition demands, set about trying to break the protective wall, to allow the bulls to escape the riders. In order to achieve this, everything, apart from blows, is allowed. Some throw buckets of water or sacks of flour on the procession, others even throw themselves at the heads of the horses, clinging to their bridles or their manes. The game is dangerous and accidents are frequent, but traditionally, they are forgotten immediately and no resentment is ever felt. If the bulls escape, the keepers have to follow them, sometimes right into the sea! However, if the 'abrivado' manages to reach the arena, it is for the keepers a day of glory. A glory sublime and joyous, and copiously toasted in the company of the followers on foot, their temporary enemies. The glory is shared with their courageous steeds.

A horseman today and no doubt tomorrow, the keeper of the Camargue is also a horseman of yesterday. He mounts a horse whose origin has been lost in the night of past centuries and millennia; he practices horsemanship which is efficient and perfectly adapted to his own country and to the demands of his livelihood; he even uses the only truly French saddle that is similar to the tournament saddle of the riders of yesteryear.

A GREAT LITTLE HORSE

From England to Norway, we meet a number of rustic horses of other breeds. For the most part they share with the Camargue horse, the limitation of their size. It is for this reason that they are often

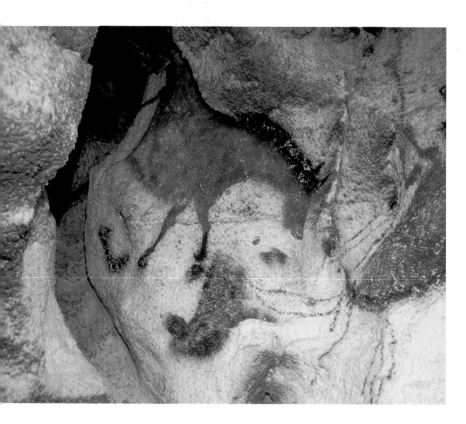

The most beautiful representations of horses in cave paintings are undoubtedly those of the caves of Lascaux (above), but those at Pech Merle (on the right), where a slightly different technique has been employed, are also interesting though less well known. The sculpting of the rock to portray the head of a horse remains one of the masterpieces of its type.

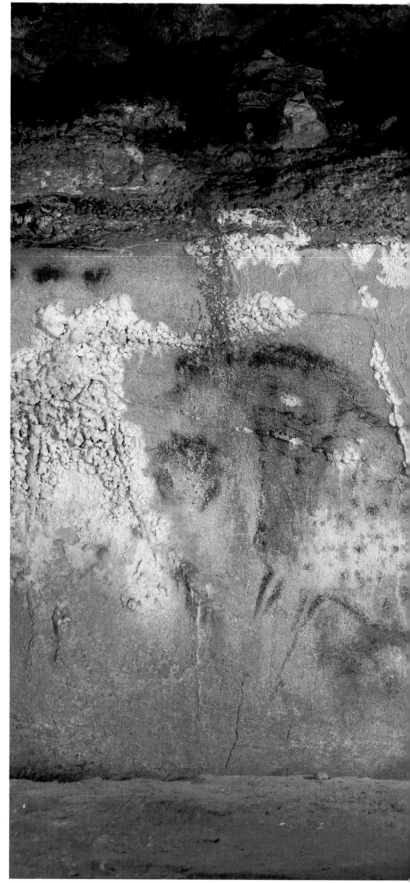

called ponies, since the official delimitation between the horse and the pony is 1.47m. However this delimitation is as arbitrary as it is absurd, for it is not uncommon to find members of the same breed with a height to the withers of more or less than 1.47m. To avoid this absurd bureaucratic distinction we will simply call them small horses.

It is the richness or the poverty of its birthplace which mainly determines the size of a breed. In general, the more meager the food, the smaller the horse. But the quality of the grass and a more or less amenable climate are parallel factors of development when it comes to its robustness and endurance: two qualities which in the past were greatly sought by man, user of the horse. So small, solid, and enduring horses, for the most part cheap to maintain and requiring little upkeep, have been throughout time assigned to the roughest tasks: moving timber on mountain slopes, pulling up carts from the bottom of mines, transporting loads along paths which are impractical for vehicles, etc.

Living, of course, in the time of the machine, the winch, and the tractor, the little horses lose, economically speaking, their reason for being. In fact, certain breed have come just a hair's breadth away from disappearing. This was the case, for example, with the ponies of the Landes, who were living wild and free in the forests of the southwest of France and in herds from which the owners of the vineyards set apart each year some horses to be especially trained and used. During the Second World War, the German troops hunted and exterminated the last of them. Descendants of small domesticated horses, today's ponies of the Landes are undoubtedly not the same as their free ancestors. Other breeds were crossed with horses of greater stature and were improved, in order to obtain a final product which is different. However, for some years or some tens of years now, a small attempt has been made across Europe to preserve the characteristics of many rustic breeds. This is because they are part of the provincial, regional and even national patrimony, or, because their specific qualities have recently opened a lucrative market for their breeders. In effect, the recent craze for the horse and horsemanship, the development of the equestrian circuit, and above all the pony clubs have led to a growing demand for rustic horses.

MINUSCULE ATHLETES

Without trying to compile a complete list of the small horses of Europe, let us briefly look at a few of them.

In France, in the Haute-Ariège, lives the semi-wild Merens, a massive, highly unusual breed, with a small heavy head. It is a zain horse, having a totally black coat without any white hairs.

Let's jump to Norway, the land of the Fjordhest. These horses were the mounts of the Vikings, whose talents were not only navigational, and whose horses have really changed very little, if at all, since that Viking time in which they were trained to fight each other! With coats of yellow-dun and grey streaks, black and white tail, and manes cut short and the black braid which circles their front legs, the Fjordhest have a slightly military look!

With a golden coat and silvery mane, the Haflinger, in Austria, is a true breed which has only been established for little more than a century. These are superb and very robust horses whose qualities are such that in 1984, after many tests, the Indian army, in order to remount their troops in the Himalayas, acquired five thousand of them!

The Shetland Isles, a minuscule part of Britain, has for the past 1,500 years been the rough, icy, barren and windswept domain of the Shetland pony.

Apart from the Falabella, a minuscule Argentinean horse, less than 70 centimeters high and the product of strict breeding, the Shetland pony in the isles of northern Scotland, with less than a metre to the withers, is the smallest horse in the world. However, considering its size, it is also the strongest! Its robustness is such that legend has it that it is capable of carrying for many miles, the family of a man who could hold it in his arms!

The ancient horseman, dressed in a light cuirass, is generally represented on a rather small and stocky horse. But do these proportions reflect the reality of the time?

Even in the West, the horse is often associated with religion: the artist of this ride of the Magi (16th century) preferred to offer them that mount rather than the usual camel.

Another leap takes us across to Iceland, the land of fire, ice, volcanoes and glaciers and an extraordinary horse which has developed over more than ten centuries in a country that is rough in the extreme. Like the Fjordhest in previous times, it was the hero of those stallion fights of which the sagas still speak. Its special attraction, the 'tolt', derived from the walk, makes for a surprisingly comfortable ride, and it has yet another quality: that of a homing pigeon! Its sense of direction is such that, if it is released far from home, it will return without any trouble at all

to its stable. In the land of more than hard winters, which cattle can not stand up to, it is raised for the saddle, the cart, the pack-saddle, or the butcher's shop.

It is extremely difficult to accept the eating of horseflesh when you love horses. However, it is to a large part thanks to it, or because of it, that in France, above all, heavyweight members of the equine breeds are still well represented.

THE TANK HORSE

As certain habitats generate small horses, others breed big ones, indeed very big ones. These latter are regions like Brabant in Belgium, Normandy and Perché in France, Lowland Scotland and the central counties of England, which have a mild climate and rich, nourishing pastures. Here are developed, often with the selective intervention of man, draught horses, which are called cold blooded.

From the Middle Ages, draught horses were used and appreciated for their capacity to carry and pull heavy loads. The pack-horse (a beast of burden, as its name implies) could easily be loaded with over one hundred kilos, which it could carry at an even pace over long distances, which was advantageous in those times when the roads were almost non-existent. Its mass and solidity allowed for the transformation of the destrier, warhorse, into a tank. Destrier means held in the right hand, or right-handed, and stems from the fact that it was always led by hand, without mounting it, saving its strength for battle and the final charge. This was a wise precaution, for at the end of the Middle Ages, a warrior in armour weighed so much that it was sometimes necessary to put him in the saddle using a hoist; what is more, the animal was often also cased in steel, from its nose to hindquarters. Having said this, in these conditions, the charge of the armored knight was in effect a slow trot over a relatively short distance, whatever the power of his horse. The invention of the arquebus, whose fire penetrated the thickest of armour, led to the disappearance of the destrier. It is believed that cavalry, in order to recover their usefulness, turned back towards the faster breeds of horse and away from the cold-

121

blooded ones which they had favoured for so long. This revolution in military equitation did not, however, mark the end of draught horses, but it would be a lengthy, and without doubt, tedious process to follow their evolution and the results of cross-breeding effected here and there by man, and the particular work to which they were put, in one region or another, at such and such a time. Whether they be Percherons, Suffolk Punches or Brabantines, throughout time they have drawn carriages, carried loads, and been harnessed to the chariot and cart, and even after the Second World War, they worked in the fields and trotted in the shafts of the vehicles

The traditional festivals of many regions associate the celebration of certain times of the year (according to the local culture) with the horse, ancient gatherer of the harvest. Games take place, as here with the Festival of Lances of Campagne (Sarthe). This is perhaps also a reminder of the knights of Antan (opposite page) and their jousts.

which took chickens, piglets, eggs, cheese, vegetables and fruit to market.

THE FUTURE RETURNS TO THE PAST

During the Fifties, draught horses were progressively replaced by the tractor and the automobile.

Many breeders of Bretons or Shires, for example, disappeared. However, breeding still carried on where heavyweight horses, no longer produced for work, were bred for the butcher's shop. If this change prevented the disappearance of certain breeds, it contributed to the transformation of the majority of them, since breeders worried more about selecting for bulk in the animal than about its aptitude or capacity for work. A revival, however, has been taking place in this area for some years. In small agricultural undertakings the tractor, as well as being costly, has shortcomings. More and more cultivators have brought back the draught horse, which pulls the hoe between rows of vines, artichokes or cauliflowers, without compressing the soil as does a machine. Above all, where leguminous crops are grown, their maintenance cost is less than the value of the manure they provide. In addition, the rapid development of trait-tract trials — races where the horse must pull a heavily laden sledge along grass or sand — provides hope that, very soon, we will once again see draught horses bred for their power and willing heart. A prickly detail is that this unusual sport is a recent import from Japan.

Let's briefly look at some specific draught horses, the largest of which, larger than any other horse, is the English Shire, whose size can reach 1.90m to the withers. The most popular in the world is the Percheron, which Americans and Japanese among others import. The most able is the Clydesdale. With his limbs covered with long white hair, he always appears to be on his way to the ball! The Poitevin has, itself, the privilege of ability to produce mules! It is the role of the Poitevin mares, covered by donkeys, to bring the mules of Poitou into the light of day. Previously famous, today only a few are in existence.

SADDLE HORSES AND WAR HORSES

After the history of country and draught horses, we turn to the saddle horses of Europe, a truly gigantic subject!

As far back as can be remembered and up until the Second World War, the last appearance of the war horse, the breeding of saddle horses has primarily been for military purposes and therefore inextricably linked to the history of arms and their development. As we have seen, the invention of the

England created a special horse, for an original sport: the horse race. This pastime of the nobility quickly became popular and the English thoroughbred was soon famous the world over.

arquebus led to the search for a type of horse other than the heavily-built Destrier, and for this, breeding was changed. In Napoleonic times (which witnessed the heyday of the cavalry as much for its panache as its efficiency), the light cavalry and the heavy cavalry needed two different types of horse: lively and fast for the Hussar, and strong and enduring for the Dragoon or the Cuirassier. These were the horses which had to be bred.

Throughout time, the production of a certain type or breed may have been encouraged by demand, but the demand for horses could not always be met. For wars and civil wars led to a major consumption of horses. In a split second, a shot or a cut with a saber could bring about the end of an animal that had taken five or six years to reach maturity. Besides, in countries ravaged by conflict, horse breeding was often impossible. All this explains why, for example, in Henry IV's time, at the end of The Hundred Year's War, up to 10,000 saddle horses a year were imported, principally from Germany, and at great expense.

It seems that up until the 19th century, every province and every region produced horses of a particular type, which were therefore easily recognizable. On this point, let us refer, by way of example to the renowned novelist Alexander Dumas who, in *The Three Musketeers*, describes the mounts of his heroes: Athos chose a superb jet black Andalusian horse; Grimaud had a Picardy horse, stocky and strong; Porthos appeared on a very fine Spanish Jennet. Mousqueton followed him on a horse from Auvergne; Aramis appeared on a superb English steed; and as for D'Artagnan's horse, it was a vigorous Mecklenburger.

Nowadays almost all horses are bred for sport and leisure, and the regional horses have seen their characteristics ironed out for the benefit of a profile or type which corresponds to the current market and riders of the consumer society. With the exception of a few mounted units, such as the English Horse Guards or the Republican Guard in France, European riders are no longer military, certainly not warriors. Their horses are today more difficult to class according to their place of origin, but they are numerous enough to give pleasure to all those who love and appreciate them.

Another sporting discipline, the cross-country event, was inspired by the training of military horses on varied terrain.

THE FASTEST AND BRIGHTEST IN THE WORLD

We can not speak about European horses and riders without referring to that phenomenon, the English thoroughbred, distinguished on the one hand, and the son of a vagabond on the other!

From the 17th century, racehorses were highly prized in England. The number of breeds where the selection was made solely in order to produce the fastest animals were numerous. Speed was the sole aim of breeding. In the 18th century, three Oriental stallions arrived in England who were coupled with

the best racing mares in the country. They were Darley Arabian, Byerley Turk and Godolphin Arabian. The history of the last of the three is to say the least curious. Sent by the Bey of Tunis to Louis XV, it was resold by him, because it was not to his taste. It was discovered in the streets of Paris, harnessed to a milk cart, by an Englishman, Lord Godolphin.

The thoroughbred, the fastest horse that exists, is descended from a cart horse, but there is no horse more famous in Europe and all over the world, for it has become the king of the racetrack, and unleashes the passions of millions of horseracing enthusiasts. Thus it has the quality of indirectly affecting the destinies of all horses and race-goers, most of whom undoubtedly never climb into a saddle. But it is, above all, the heart of a notable breed (the most important in the world), which, in view of recent performances, is destined to improve consistently like pure breed, as it is cross-bred with more natural stock, in order to refine certain sporting characteristics. This is, however, only a repetition of what was done for the sake of improvement, with

the Oriental horse, and had already been done in Spain before that, in order to create that shining example of the equine breed, the Andalusian horse.

ANDALUSIA, WHERE EQUESTRIAN ART WAS CREATED

The Spanish peninsula, endowed from the outset with the same equine breed as Northern and Western Europe, benefited from two factors, one climatic and the other religious, which transformed its horse breeding and gave it an international significance. First of all, the climate, which varies greatly from the fertile North to the South with its tendency towards semi-aridity, helped to create well-tempered and enduring horses, on the basis of qualities

Preceding pages: In Spain the festival is still a valued opportunity to ride a horse in ceremonial costume. Some Andalusians are thus emboldened to wear the caballero costume.

Spanish equestrian history was influenced by the Arabs; it was only five centuries ago that the Moors were chased from their last strongholds in Spain.

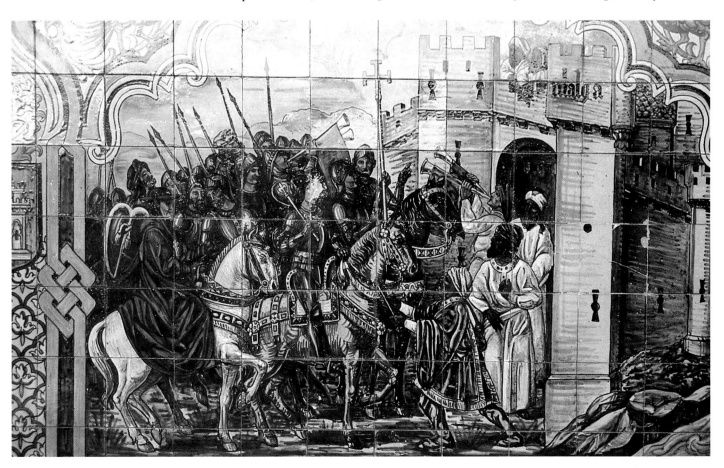

The inimitable gift of the caballeros must be the noble look and the docile character of their horse. The Andalusian horse gives its rider (whatever sex or age) the agreeable impression of travelling in the company of a friend.

inherited from their Nordic antecedents. But the Moorish invasion, and the Islamic culture which was imposed for many centuries (from the 8th to the 15th century over the most southern provinces) established a refined Oriental breed and a new equestrian culture. In effect, the heat, as much as the superiority of the Arab light cavalry persuaded the Spanish horsemen of the ineffective and illusory aspects of protection by heavy armour. This was a tendency which the invention of gunpowder helped to establish early on in Europe, and which the Spanish cavalry had anticipated by several decades. At the same time, this orientation towards a more refined equestrian technique required the mount itself to be more mobile and faster than the Destrier. Until then there had been opposition to the Arab horse but cross-breeding (usually of the Barbary breed) with the indigenous horses, was inevitable despite the Islamic principles of pure breeding, and tended to produce offspring which were robust and fast, and with much heart and panache. This well-matched breeding was to create the Andalusian horse.

This special horse, responding to particular needs, is perhaps the first successful example of planned cross-breeding between two radically different equine stocks. The new possibilities of this mount served a new and more refined horsemanship, with evasive tactics, and unprecedented military parades and maneuvers. This revolution, soon carried around the world by the horsemen of Castille and Aragon, had a profound influence on Western Europe. Out of it was born the Italian academies, whose masters were soon outshone by their pupils, the French. At this point we could mention Solomon of La Broue and Pluvinel, who turned the precepts of the Neapolitans Grisone and Pignatelli into an art form; or we could recall the worldwide influence of the teaching of the Frenchman, La Guérinière, who will remain at the heart of academic horsemanship, which is an idea as much as a way of mounting a horse. All the great equestrian schools of today (the Cadre Noir in Saumur, the Spanish school in Vienna, and even the Andalusian School of Equestrian Art) embody the continuity of his teaching. The Andalusian horse will for a long time be the basis of that horsemanship. Docile, manageable, alert and robust, it will permit horsemen to increase

All shapes and colours, the dress of the Andalusian is in some ways a counterpoint to the equestrian severity of the horseman.

The chariot which carries an effigy of the Virgin of Rocio, with two of the riders who accompany the faithful.

their original skills, by reexamining the movements of equestrian combat. These famous noble skills, taught today by the great schools, are the aesthetic versions of defensive movements which previously were used save the rider from gunfire or the saber.

Replaced in the French Higher School by the English horse, the Andalusian horse, by way of compensation, gave birth to the famous lipizzaner, the white horse of the School of Vienna, called Spanish in honour of this line of descent. The Iberian horse, therefore, still sets the pace for academic horsemanship, all the more since the Andalusian School, situated at Jerez, the third traditional conservatory along with the Cadre Noir and the Viennese School, is again mounted exclusively on horses of the region.

THE ANDALUSIAN RIDER: BETWEEN WORK AND PLAY

We have drifted away somewhat from daily life. The term 'conservatoire' might tend to make you think that the Spanish horse exists only in museums. Nothing could be further from the truth, for in the same way as the draught horse still works in the rich vineyards of the region (the sherry of Jerez has been exported throughout the entire world, notably by the English who are very much wine lovers), the Andalusian horse is still essential to man in his relations with bulls, and participates more than ever in religious and non-religious festivals. Here it contributes to an indispensable figure at these gatherings, the caballero, proud, assured, and certainly a little macho, but who in fact places much value on the beautiful Andalusian horse with its gypsy coat.

The most striking example of this horsemanship present in daily life is of course found in Andalusia. This is the place of pilgrimage of the Rocio, which carries the hernandades (religious brotherhood) through more than sixty towns to the church Notre-Dame-du-Rocio in the village of the same name, in the magnificent national park between Jerez, Seville and Huelva. The aim of every community is to take its effigy of the Blessed Virgin Mary to hail the statue which, having been stolen by some looters after the retreat of the Moors, had been lost during a battle in the Marshlands, and was found again later by a shepherd after a revelation. Several miracles established the popularity of the pilgrimage, and for many years the Spanish queen herself has participated in this cavalcade of several days, accompanied by one or another of the brotherhood.

But the festival has grown well beyond its religious aspect, with its campfires around which the dancers get tipsy at every stop, the parades of caballeros in festival costume, seated on the hind-quarters, with or without Andalusian dignity, and the pride of the riders showing off their most beautiful horses. The superb Andalusian horses walk or gallop a great part of the way along the procession, from the vehicle carrying the banner of the Blessed Virgin, at the head, right back to the rear which consists of family, bedding, and food for the three or four days of the pilgrimage. All this is lubricated by the famous sherry. Perhaps the dust raised by hooves makes one thirsty! But the caballero always remains dignified, and having arrived, his Andalusian horse still parades in the streets of Rocio, before and after the long religious ceremony (followed on horseback

Both a religious pilgrimage and a pagan festival, the pardon of the Virgin of the Rocio is a chance for the inhabitants of Huelva, Seville and the surrounding areas to show off their most beautiful horses either harnessed in the Andalusian way or drawing decorated wagons.

On the roads of the village of Rocio, each 'hernandad' (religious brotherhood) parade in order to escort the Virgin to the church. During the whole of Saturday the corteges follow one another, then in the evening, each caballero remounts his Andalusian horse on the crupper and trots through in the dust for a tour of the village, and to meet with his friends.

by many). Old acquaintances join together for the occasion and visit one another, and the long journey on horseback is spent talking, drinking and nibbling food (always in the saddle); so ends this unusual religious festival.

Of course, the Rocio is not a weekly event, but the opportunity to ride is easily found in Andalusia, not only on Sundays, but also on market days, etc. The horse is too important for its rider not to share the daily work; the festival is also for the horse (perhaps more so) as well as for his rider. Like the rider, brought up with the corrida, the horse is entitled to great attention and to the most elaborate training (after all the life of the rider depends on it), and still basks in this whole region in the tradition of honour. And even if horsemanship has followed the evolution of society towards a codification of methods previously considered natural, it remains, in Andalusia perhaps more than anywhere else, an important part of social life.

It is in order to pay homage to this continuity that we have not placed this country and its horses alongside the equestrian traditions of North Africa (despite the influence of the Moors), but at the end of Europe and at the beginning of the Americas, the New World which it was given to the Iberian horse to conquer.

133

FROM THE CONQUISTADORS TO THE CHARROS

RETURN TO THE CRADLE

Setting off in search of the Indies, Christopher Columbus did not discover what is today called America, but only a small island in the Bahamas: Guanahani. Moreover, this was not his only mistake, since for a long time he remained convinced that the horse was native to the lands he had discovered. We are told, in his letters to the King of Spain, that the natives of the shores of Panama had horses which they used in battle. As everybody knows, this was not so, but it could have been true, since distant ancestors of the horse, from the eohippus to the equus, had developed over millions of years on the new continent before they mysteriously disappeared during the Ice Age. (The different hypotheses advanced to explain this disappearance such as epidemics, migration, predatory action, etc., are all plausible, but not verifiable.)

The importation of horses to the New World, where none were to be found, and then the breeding of them, was the task to which Columbus and those who were to follow him first applied themselves. A royal decree, dated May 23rd, 1493, is proof of this: '. . . along with the other people, who we order to leave, will be sent twenty lancers and their horses

The Peruvian horsemen wear an ample costume, the folds of which can flap behind them in a rather disagreeable way. But it is not important, thanks to the particularly comfortable gait (the paso) which their horses adopt and which allows them to remain saddled without fatigue.

and five of them must take two horses, these two horses being mares'. The vessels referred to in this decree were those of Columbus, on the eve they set sail on their second crossing of the Atlantic. The order for five cavaliers to take mares, at a time when hardly anything but stallions were ridden, clearly demonstrates the royal desire to see stud farms created in the newly discovered lands.

In 1498, Columbus set out on a further voyage and this time his vessels had forty cavalrymen and their horses on board. Three years later, Don Nicolas de Ovando crossed the water with eighteen other animals of good stock. This is about the most exact information that we have at our disposal with regard to the number of animals that were transported from one continent to the other. Although others were later brought from Spain, for example, 106 mares in 1507, the number was very limited since at that time there was a real shortage of horses in the Iberian peninsula. So, twenty-five, plus forty, plus eighteen, and a few more, adds up to very little (especially since losses sustained during the crossings were an average of 50%). Yet it was this meager number of livestock which was, for the most part, the origin of the surprising and formidable equine population of the American continent.

It began with the stud farms set up by the settlers who arrived in the first caravels. Initially in Haiti and then in Cuba, horses multiplied very quickly, so well in fact that in just a few decades, the price of a horse fell from 500 pesos of gold (a colossal sum, justified by the horses' rarity) to 4 or 5 pesos. A hundred times less! In 1519, Cortez set foot in the land which was to become Mexico and, for the first time, put ashore on the continent a group of horses, which were as incongruous as they were laughable: stallions and mares, including some foals, bays, grays and piebalds. In all, there were sixteen animals who, as auxiliaries to their masters, set out to conquer this New World, one of the cradles of their species. In the same way as their horses, the riders were to pursue this conquest unaided.

This engraving of 1579 shows the surrender of the Indians, who are lined up like beasts of burden before the power of one Spanish horseman. It was only after having seen the first dead bodies of a horse that the inhabitants of these lands, where the horse was unknown, were persuaded that those who mounted the horse were not gods. But it was too late for their civilization, destroyed by a handful of conquistadors.

HORSES OR GODS

Despite their very small number, the horses of the conquistadors were to be one of their greatest assets in making a success of their foolhardy venture: the appropriation of an empire of eleven million inhabitants (the conquistadors numbered only 508). At the sight of the quadrupeds the Indians were immediately terrified and the strange creatures were elevated to the status of gods. As fine horsemen, knowing perfectly the psychology of the horse, the Spanish were not going to miss this chance of exploiting the credulity of the natives.

Forty Indian chiefs presented themselves at the Spanish camp in order to negotiate. First, a cavalry parade was staged for their benefit and they were highly impressed by the extent to which the bearded men mastered the gods. However they were much

Times have changed, but is this little horse on the bonnet of a car just a decoration or is it also a bringer of good luck?

he realized that the stallion, having a splinter in its foot, could not make the smallest step. Fearing for his life, he resolved to abandon his horse there and then, which he proceeded to do. Morzillo was truly to become a god: a century later, two priests were shocked to discover his statue in the largest temple in the city, where he was worshiped under the name of Tzimincher.

Obviously, the credulity of the Indians could only last for a while, and they very quickly learnt how to get to know the horse and to appreciate it as a mount, and as food!

TOO MANY MUSTANGS TO COUNT

The region of Mexico having been conquered, Spanish explorers set out towards the north in search of the mythical seven fabulous cities, crammed with gold and silver. It was in this way that the horse became known to the Indian and first set foot on the immense American desert. Then the religious orders took a hand and led the horse from Chihuahua to Texas and from New Mexico to California where they established numerous (but sometimes short-lived) missions.

In 1540, Coronado set out at the head of an expedition consisting of, among others, 240 riders. This lasted two and a half years, and went as far as what is today Kansas. It was a route as long as it was difficult, but over the decades it was to be followed by many other treasure hunters, such as Juan de Onate (1596), and Juan de Anza (1774), who opened up the arduous California route. Everyone travelled by horse, and more or less everyone got lost or was pillaged by the Indians.

It was in order to evangelize the Indians and to encourage colonization that, following the explorers, Franciscans, Jesuits and Dominicans set up, further and further north, a considerable number of missions. The existence of these establishments was supported by farming and stock-raising, above all of cattle, imported from Spain. However, across the wide open spaces totally without enclosures or fences, vaqueros (herdsmen on horseback) were needed to guard and move the herds. Despite their fears of seeing the Indians become riders, and by

more impressed with the stallion who, held by hand, suddenly advanced towards them, nostrils dilated, looking furious and stamping the ground violently with its front hooves: the god was showing them his anger! The Indians were evidently a long way from guessing that, in order to get the horse to behave like that, the wily Cortez had simply concealed a mare in heat behind them!

In Mexico, Cortez, in the saddle, carried by the god, paid a visit to the emperor Montezuma. It was an impressive spectacle for the Aztec sovereign, which he viewed from a convenient distance! In 1524, Cortez arrived just outside the city Maya in Tayasal. The natives discovered, with disbelief and terror, the animals of the conquistadors. Trembling with fear, they invited Cortez to visit their town riding on his black stallion, Morzillo. But at dawn, when the conqueror decided to return to his camp,

consequence formidable warriors, the Spanish, too few in number to take on the job of looking after the herds, were gradually forced to teach the equestrian art to the natives (or rather to let them learn it themselves). These natives rapidly became expert horsemen and it was not unusual for them, tired of a life of servitude, to flee, and return to their tribes taking horses and cattle with them. These tribes, having had the vaqueros as teachers, were very shortly to take their turn in discovering the equestrian science and in eating the horse in times of famine. Next, they mounted raids to steal new horses from the missions, often letting loose part of their plunder on the way back. These horses which were set free were the first of the wild mustangs which, over many centuries, became too numerous to count.

IN SPITE OF THE IRON HORSE

For a long time, the New Spain extended its immense territories, taking in modern Mexico and the southwest of the United States; and for a long time, across these arid stretches, struggles persisted between white men and Indians, Mexicans and Americans, Mexicans and French, as well as others. It would be tedious to list these multiple battles, of varying importance, or the staggering marches or countermarches which preceded them and brought them about. But in almost all these events, horses and cavalry played their part.

In 1848, at the end of a bitter two-year struggle, the United States imposed the frontiers on Mexico which we know today. However, across the sierras and the deserts dotted with cactus, the warrior horsemen pursued each other for decades, including those who defeated a French expeditionary corps sent by Napoleon III, those of the famous Pancho Villa and his horse Seven Leagues, and those of the no less famous Zapata. This was the period when the railway (the iron horse appeared, shortly followed by the steam-horse or automobile, but neither one nor

The architecture and the skill with which this stable seems to have been built recall the great Spanish breeding stables, but the equestrian habits here are very different.

138

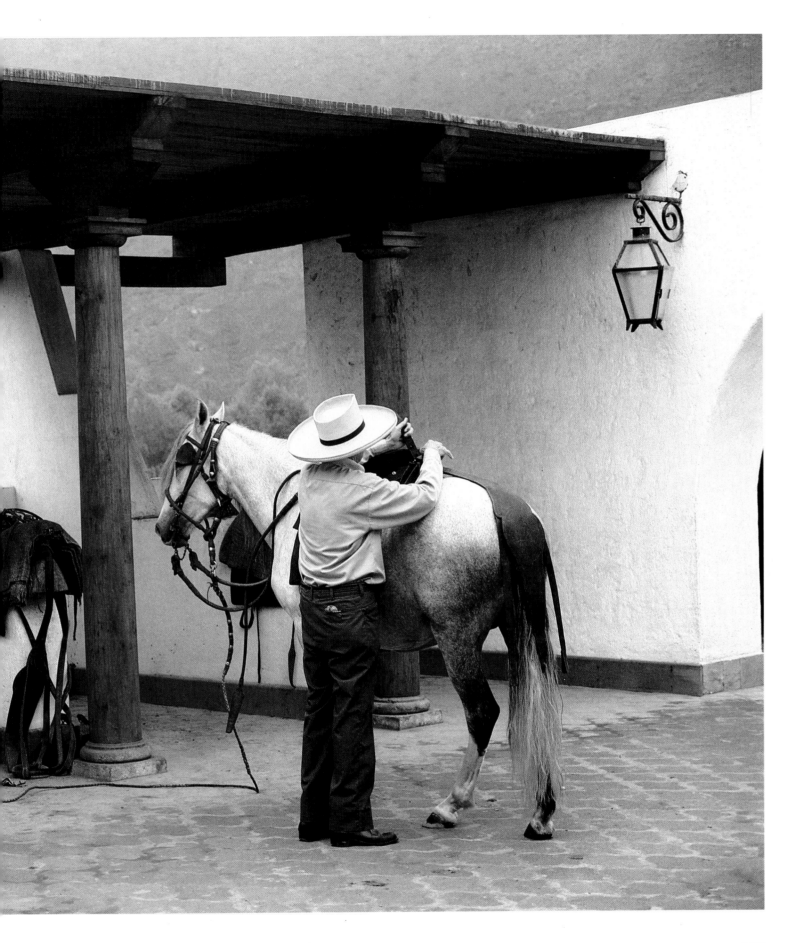

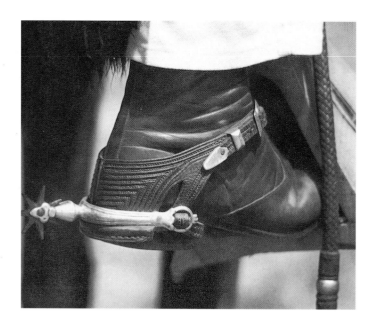

Included among the tests, or games most often held in a charreria, are the paso de muerte in which the player has to jump, barefoot, from one horse to another and the suerte de colear in which the rider must pursue a bull, grab hold of its tail and bring it to the ground. During these exercises the horses are rarely spared, and brutal collisions, demanded by convention, are frequent. The charro is a more primitive rider than a true horseman. He is heavy-

It is difficult to appreciate the practicality of these spurs and saddle when one sees how finely worked they are. But the horse still plays a part in daily life in Latin America, and a good worker needs to have the best tools possible.

the other, until recent times, managed to totally supplant the horse of flesh and bone which has always been omnipresent in Mexican life.

THE CHARRO: A MACHO RIDER

In Mexico, the subject of the horse is almost synonymous with that of the charro. This charro is what all the riders, of the country, young and old, dream of being. Charro is simply a noble title for the horseman, and one can be recognised even when he is dismounted. With a bronzed face under the wide brim of a sombrero, he walks with the step of someone more used to travelling on four feet than two. The pistol at his side is less impressive than his assured look and pride; his haughty air is the epitome of machismo. He is a lord who would not let another pass first, but a lord whose total worth very often consists only of his equestrian talents and his taste for danger. In the saddle he seems even stronger, conquering, and an equal to the gods put ashore in his country four centuries ago.

The charreria is the show in which the charro demonstrates the measure of his talents as a rider. Created by the necessities of cattle ranching, it is at the same time a stylish game and spectacle, which generally takes place in an arena. It is fast, violent and brutal.

In the Andes, there is no horse breeding; only adventurous travellers take the risk of going there where water may be frozen on a summers day.

handed, and uses his spurs readily, but he is also the king of the lasso, which he calls a reata. It is with unequaled dexterity that he captures, always at a gallop, a calf or mule by the front (mangana) or back (piala) legs. Whilst performing these two feats of skill, certain charros, concerned to demonstrate their skill and their scorn of the risk, do not hesitate to do it on foot with the end of the lasso fixed to their neck! It is a spectacle to make you shiver! As for the floreo, it is similar to a circus act, and consists of using the loop of the reata to depict circles, arabesques, and movements as gracious and vivid as they are impressive. Some practice this floreo on horseback, some even standing up on their saddle! There are about 350 charros associations currently in existence, which shows to what extent the charreria is popular. For the charro, the day of rest, which he turns into a festival day, is in reality not at all restful, and when the charreria is

finished, he returns to the humble and less glorious tasks of the vaquero which are more often his business. Whether he works on a modest ranch or on a large and rich hacienda, abandoning his Sunday costume — the showy sombrero and the silver spurs —, he climbs into the saddle again in order to push, pull and round up the cattle.

In love with this voluntary display, even if it is absurd, the charro is before all else macho for him the horse is a means of showing off his virility and sheer strength. This state of mind determines what sort of rider he is and will remain, whatever the extent of the invasion of the horse-power engine.

141

TO THE COUNTRY

OF THE WESTERN

An Indian is seen on horseback in profile against a backdrop which has been the setting for many Westerns. This impressive landscape is appropriately named Monument Valley.

Hunting bison was the main occupation of the tribes of the plains and provided them with the essentials of their daily life. Escaped and returned to the wild, captured or stolen from the white man, the horse made the hunt easier for these instinctive horsemen.

THE CALIFORNIANS:
A PEOPLE IN THE SADDLE

The history of North American horses and horsemen is so complex that it can be tackled in a multitude of ways. Contrary to what is most often done, we are going to study its evolution, not from east to west, but from the Pacific to the Atlantic. We shall start with California, which was for a long time Mexican, without being truly assimilated. The route between Mexico and California, opened by Juan de Anza in 1774, was cut off a few years later by the Yuma Indians, who were embittered by the actions of the white men. No longer connected to Mexico except by way of the sea, the California colony developed almost in isolation, trapped by the deserts in the south, the Rockies in the east, and the Pacific in the west. The mildness of the climate and the richness of the land favoured the birth of a pastoral society, and as such, a people of horsemen. The country was gigantic and the population was thinly scattered (6,000 souls, of which there were only 2,000 men at the start of the colony!). The rearing of livestock,

mainly cattle, was practiced on enormous properties, and as far as one can judge, in about 1830, the number of livestock on the Vallejo hacienda was 50,000 cattle, 25,000 sheep and 8,000 horses, living on 125,000 hectares! The only way the few hundred men employed by the establishment could manage to move across such an immense land and work with the cattle, was on horseback. So Californians spent the greater part of their lives in the saddle. Men, women and children chose their mounts from immense herds, descendants of the first horses brought by the Spanish and returned to the wild. Everyone was a horse rider, and an American was able to write of these people: 'If they could go on horseback

into the sea and fish from the height of their saddle, they would often be seen breaking through the waves; instead, they show themselves to be incapable of standing up in a boat.'

The horsemanship of the Californian vaquero and the harnessing of his horse were very special, since it was influenced at the same time by the Spanish tradition and by the requirements of the country. It is from the vaquero that the Anglo-Saxons who came from the east, borrowed techniques and equipment, in order to become cowboys or cowhands in their turn. However before reaching the blessed land of California, where the people lived like princes, they had to cross the plains and mountains and face the

Red Indian, the Redskin whose life was changed by the advent of the horse.

THE REDSKIN AND THE CIVILIZATION OF THE HORSE

Up until the 17th century, when he discovered the horse, the Red Indian corresponded very little with the image which has been portrayed in so many westerns. The majority of tribes led a sedentary existence and the most gentle of lives. Fishing, hunting, gathering fruits and flowers, they nonetheless did not always manage to avoid famine at the end of the winter.

Only a few tribes of the plains, such as the Comanches, Apaches, and Arapahos, lived a nomadic life following the bison, which served their most important needs. It was not easy for people on foot to hunt these enormous animals, and the methods employed were risky. They consisted, for example, of approaching the herd on all fours, disguised by a wolf's skin, in order to try and shoot a stone-tipped arrow, or attracting a herd on to the top of a cliff and stampeding it in such a way that it would rush headlong into a ravine. Once the hunt finished, if it had some success, the nomads only had one draught animal of value to bring the game back to their camp, and this was the dog, which they loaded up or harnessed to a light sledge because of its small size, it could only carry or pull small loads.

Then came the horse. Having escaped and returned to the wild, having been stolen from the white man and sold by one tribe to another, in two and a half centuries the horse spread throughout the continent, between Mexico and Canada. No doubt the tribes, never having seen horsemen, thought at first that the horse was a new type of game. Then it was used mainly to replace the dog for carrying or pulling loads. Finally it was mounted, and totally transformed the Indian way of life; they became remarkable horsemen.

To be on horseback was to be fast and mobile. For the nomads hunting became much easier, even if it did demand great skill, and consequently famine

became rare on the plains where bisons roamed by the million. Sedentary peoples, such as the Sioux and the Cheyennes, set about leading a nomad existence, invading the territory of other tribes, and fighting them, and thus changing their lives in areas as diverse as food, habitat and crafts. Changing from farming to hunting, they got used to an abundant diet of meat and had at their disposal quantities of skins. Thanks to these skins, they built larger teepees and tents which the horses were able to pull on sledges constructed with long poles which constituted their framework and which carried the weight of the tent itself. Again the abundance of furs permitted them to dress differently (without doubt better), as well as to put together the harnesses they needed. These harnesses, as well as their horses, were very often gaily decorated. The decorations of the latter — feathers, paint, etc. — had in many

Trappers also hunted bison. The gun permitted methods of approach less risky than those practiced by the Red Indians and led to the massacre of innumerable herds of these animals. It was one of the causes of the first confrontations between 'white' and 'red' men, the latter claiming less the possession of land than the right to live according to their customs and to subsist on the product of their hunts.

horses and it was vital to procure mounts in the absence breeding them. Nowadays, the Navajos, for example, still leave their horses to reproduce in the freedom of their immense reservation in Arizona and sequester the best of the herds, leaving the more mediocre to reproduce. Today, the Navajos are more generally horse breeders than horse thieves.

Among the rare peoples who have shown themselves to be good selectors and shrewd horse breeders, let us look at the Nez-Percés. In their mountains in Oregon and Idaho, they developed a breed of horses that are mottled and very fast, called Appaloosas, named after a river near where they live: the Palouse. Discovering these animals at the beginning of the 19th century, the explorers Lewis and Clark judged them equal or superior to any that could be found on the pastures of Virginia. A fine compliment for a fine horse.

THE BEST LIGHT CAVALRY IN THE WORLD

A man close to nature, as well as an observer and connoisseur of animal life by necessity, the American Indian handled the horse with care and gentleness. Far from trying to subdue or restrain the bronco, the unbroken horse, he tried to convince it that his presence was not only not dangerous, but that it could even be agreeable. Two of the methods he employed to achieve this, were, first, he made the horse go into water up to its shoulders before mounting it, and thus made it incapable of any sudden movement, the horse very quickly realised that the presence of the man on his back was of no risk at all to him, and second, the oldest method of the horse school master, known to all riding people. The schoolmaster is an old, calm horse, whose presence calms the pupil and who serves as an example to follow.

cases, a meaning. Some were meant to praise the animal for qualities such as speed; others were proof of victories or outstanding actions in which it had participated.

The social role of the horse sprang from the importance that it had in moving about, hunting and waging war. It meant wealth and therefore was a form of exchange money or compensation. In the majority of tribes, a suitor offered horses to the family of his future wife and there is the famous case of Chief Blackfoot who, in order to get elected the leader of his people, gave away all the horses he stole from other clans.

Stealing horses was a sport which for a long time was the passion of the Red Indian tribes. Up until the beginning of this century, if we are to believe certain sources, this theft was caused by one simple reason: few Red Indians were interested in rearing

Two aspects of North American equestrian tradition which persist today: on the one hand, a descendant of the great Crow warriors who lives on a reservation and wears the festival costume of his ancestors, but rides a horse whose bridle bit is not Indian at all. On the other hand, the far-reaching line of a herd of cattle driven as in past centuries by horsemen with leather chaps and wide-brimmed hats.

148

More than the horses' great qualities, it was this gentle education which explains the stunning performances which the Indian was able to achieve with his horse. He rode it bareback and guided it more with his legs than with the cord which passed around the horse's lower jaw instead of a bridle. This, method was generally used for hunting bison with a bow and arrow, which required the use of two hands, and with the lance which involved getting very near to the animal. In order to achieve such feats with such minimal hold and guidance, understanding and total cooperation between man and his mount were necessary.

Despite his equestrian ability, the Indian did not scorn the saddle, which was particularly comfortable when making long journeys. He manufactured it, as we have seen, but he also stole it when he got the chance, or even bought it. Thus in about 1890, Nino Cochise, the Apache Chief, after he had remounted his warriors, had the chore of taking home a Mexican saddler from which he bought several dozen saddles. However primitive, the Red Indian rider was not adverse to comfort!

When we consider the equestrian skills of the majority of the Indians, we can understand how the white men, invading their territories and facing them in battle, sometimes called them red devils and sometimes admired them as forming the best light cavalry in the world.

THE WHITE INVASION

It was during the 19th century that, from the east, white men spread across the whole of the North American continent. Explorers — Lewis, Clark, Pike and others —, missionaries, and trappers, many of them Frenchmen who came from Canada, were the first to open up the mountain passes, plains and deserts. Then came the Gold Rush and the onslaught on the Far West and its lands, ripe for appropriation. On their long and arduous progress towards the promised land, the emigrants brought a certain number of horses from east to west, from New England to Oregon, California or New Mexico. Of European stock, these animals, brought from France, England and Sweden since the 17th century — could bring little new blood into the great desert, since only a limited number of them were able to reach that far. The pioneers who followed the Santa Fe trail or the Bozeman Trail were for the most part poor people whose means did not permit them to have numerous mounts. As for their covered wagons, which so many bad films show being pulled by horses, they were in general drawn by cattle — sometimes by mules, which, although slower, were more economical, and hardier than horses.

Although they brought few horses into the West, the newcomers found enough of them there to start horse-rearing on the immense open pastures. The special requirements of this activity led to the birth of a figure whose image — often distorted — was to travel the world: the cowboy.

FROM THE VAQUERO TO THE COWBOY

It was in Texas, on the edge of the Mexican frontier and above all in California, virtually self-sufficient for a decade, that the colonists discovered the vast potential for rearing livestock offered by the untouched spaces of the West. There, since the Spanish conquest and the establishment of the missions, the vaquero tended herds of cattle, not so much for the meat, but more for the profitable tallow and leather trade. Determined to make a dollar, the Anglo-Saxons took to rearing livestock with great efficiency and the aim of supplying the markets in the East with live cattle which were easy to sell at a high price. (In 1876, the mid-east of the United States had 42 million inhabitants against only two million in the west.) In order to guard and manage these immense herds, they had to either become cowboys or to employ them.

If there was a need to prove all that the cowboy owes to the vaquero, it is enough to compare the vocabulary used in common to describe their equipment and aspects of their horses. Thus, the chappareras of the vaquero, leather or skin trousers, protection against the ropes and thorns are called chaps by the cowboy; the sombrero, above all in the South, is the sombrero; a pinto horse is a pinto; etc., etc. Emulating the vaquero, it seems that in many

cases the cowboy has surpassed his model in dexterity and efficiency. He very quickly learnt how to adapt to the rugged terrain of the country which he had made his own and to the type of horsemanship that was required by his diverse tasks, often boring and monotonous — much less romantic than you might imagine.

Whether he was the owner of a modest ranch and a few hundred head of cattle, or worked on one of the great ranges (hundreds or even millions of hectares), the cowboy's job consisted of much besides those adventurous long journeys of which horsemen all over the world dream. Before all else he was a cowhand, and his first concern was the cattle.

He had to care for them, dress their wounds and infected brands, and cut the horns of the longhorns to prevent them from wounding one another. When he discovered one stuck in the mud, he pulled it out of its unfortunate predicament by means of his lasso

tied round the pommel of his saddle. In times of drought, he sometimes labored across many miles to create fire-breaks. However, the outbreaks of fire were not unusual. In winter, even though the snow was very deep, he patrolled and drove the pregnant cows through the cold to places sheltered by the wind where grass was available. On these occasions, he saved many small calves by carrying them across his saddle. For some of these activities his horse was a collaborator, for others, simply a means of locomotion.

The cowboy's horse in the 1850's was called the cow pony. A hybrid with a very strong percentage

The prototype of the cowboy! With his hat and his face chiselled by the land and the weather, he rides to accompany a herd, or to bring back a stray beast in a blizzard. You're not going to tell him that the helicopter or the four-wheel-drive is more up to date.

of Mustang blood, it lived in the wild until five years of age, when it was captured and broken in. In a few hours, and by force, a specialist taught the horse to respect and fear man.

This violent method, uncommon today, was employed in preference to the gentle and efficient methods favoured by the Indians for economic reasons. The work, as incessant as it was varied, did not allow the cowboy himself to train a horse, which required patience and, above all, time. However, the cowhand who was assigned — or who bought — a horse broken in this way, which was still stubbornly disobedient and knew nothing of the work for which it was destined, had every interest in understanding his horse as much as possible.

For the two of them were going to live together and face the cold, ice, snow, heat, drought and thirst. On more than one occasion, the cowboy would have to trust his life to the adroitness and instinct of his mount: he would rely on it to detect and avoid drifting sand, or even to escape a stampede. And then, throughout the long and solitary watches, which could last for months, in cabins far from the

152

ranch, the only company for man was his horse. As Jim Christian, a Texan cowboy noted: 'My horse is my friend. For you can spend much time patting and currying your horse and joking with him'.

Cows, hard work, desolate wide open spaces, solitude, but also the horse: this is what filled the rough life of the cowboy.

THE ROUNDUPS AND THE CATTLE DRIVES

Only two enterprises offered the cowboy the opportunity to pass all his days in the saddle and to demonstrate his endurance and his riding ability: the roundup, the annual gathering together of the cattle, and the long drive, convoying the herds over long distances. In both cases the job was so tiring that he could not ride his favorite horse continually, when he had one, for he daily wore out many mounts.

To carry out a roundup, dozens, indeed hundreds, of cowboys were necessary. From sunrise, under the direction of the foreman or the owner, the team of riders encircled a specific piece of territory, making their way towards the centre to which they herded the cattle dispersed in canyons, at water holes or in the grasslands. Interspersed with brief pursuits to recover those who got away, the cowhands followed behind the mooing beasts down sheer slopes, across unfertile outback, and along the paths of creeks. When, towards midday, the whole of the selected area had been combed, and a herd had been rounded up, the yearly branding of the calves commenced. It was then that the cutting horse came on the scene, surprising in its capacity to work alone, on a simple sign from his rider. The man and his mount slowly penetrated, step by step, into the herd. As soon as the cowboy had picked out a calf to capture, he showed it to his horse, then he slackened the reins and left the matter to the horse's own initiative.

Calmly, but sometimes biting it, the animal separated the little calf from the herd and then prevented it from returning. How? By following it, nose to the ground, in the same way as a dog. And this continued until its rider had lassoed the calf's back legs and led it to the place where the brand of its owner was applied.

Subtle, gentle and capable of great concentration — qualities resulting only from a judicious training — the good cutting horse was the horse that every true cowboy dreamed of possessing.

The roundup was the prelude to the long drive. In Texas, hundreds, often thousands, of head of cattle were gathered together and driven over three or four months, up to Kansas where they were loaded onto wagons destined for Chicago, the central market for meat. Guided by a trail leader, the convoy was made up of a variable number of cowboys — one for every 250 to 400 beasts —, a remuda, a herd of replacement horses led by a wrangler and a chuck wagon containing the cook and provisions.

The slow and monotonous advance behind a herd mooing and kicking up clouds of dust from which the cowboy protected himself by means of a scarf called a bandanna — was punctuated by incidents, accidents and difficult passages. Cattle thieves were often lying in wait for the drives. Indians also, who

A long way from their state on the day of departure, this is what chaps, boots and spurs look like after the drive

tried less to attack the convoy than to extort payment for right of way, or to beg an ox. Nature was hostile, with gigantic storms, and formidable downpours of hailstones as big as eggs. Wading through rivers was easy, but swimming was less so. And then there were rivers which it was absolutely imperative to stop the herd from drinking because of the alkaline water. The solution was to launch into a full gallop in order to pass it. Let us imagine the ride! Crossing the deserts was a real test. In order to complete a certain stage of the journey, the cowboys sometimes had to remain in the saddle for dozens of hours at a stretch, without closing an eye. Lack of sleep was their lot throughout the long drive, since every night they had to take turns watching the herd. They then saddled their night horse, sure of foot, not worried by the shadows or by isolated sounds or movements. Two of them, at walking pace, toured around the multitude of animals which were more or less asleep, singing or playing the harmonica to lull them. What was not always prevented was the triggering

of a fierce stampede, the sudden and unforeseen flight of the whole herd, which had to be pursued in full darkness, at a wild gallop, as it was essential to recapture the cattle before they had scattered. One can only imagine the sense of relief felt when this wave of animals was finally halted.

It was for a poor salary that the cowboy, for months on end, withstood these tests and ran all these risks (very often the price of a new pair of boots). On the whole they did it for the love of the job.

The grand era of drives came to an end in the 1880's, after having lasted less than thirty years. Civilization had made great strides by then. River-ways were extended. Barbed-wire fences and wind-

155

Teamwork is also seen at the rodeo: one of the riders controls the calf's direction, whilst the other jumps at the gallop, on to the bull calf to immobilise it and bring it down.

Right: Modern life is not an obstacle for the drivers of herds. Horses drive the cattle through towns and traffic.

mills (to draw water from the wells) made their appearance. The saga of the Wild West came to an end. Yet it still lives on.

This is proven by the success achieved at the beginning of this century across the entire world by the famous equestrian show of Buffalo Bill, the Wild West Show; the craze led to innumerable Westerns (good and bad), a passion for horsemanship, and the rodeo loved by so many Americans.

With the approach of the year 2000, the cowboy no longer has much in common with his rough forefathers. But he still conserves their spirit, and he is always a horseman.

BETWEEN THE COMPUTER AND THE LEGEND OF THE WEST

New Mexico is pink and pastel green country, with its plains as immense as they are dry, desolate and uninhabited. Standing on a mesa (rocky plateau)

the buildings of a ranch are scattered around a cluster of trees rising up beside a spring. A landing strip of beaten earth lies near them. A small airplane lands, from which wriggles out a man who only vaguely looks like a pilot. Dressed in jeans, wearing a large felt hat and pointed boots, he is every bit a cowboy. Leaving his aircraft, he makes his way towards a corral where he saddles a solid quarter horse and puts saddle-packs on half a dozen mules which he loads with four blocks of salt each. Do you imagine that he is going to mount his horse and lead the beasts of burden? Not at all! He guides this four-footed entourage to a long truck, he opens the door, and the horse and mules calmly enter without a bridge. Then without bothering to tether the harnessed animals who choose the position in the vehicle which suits them best, he takes the wheel of the truck and drives off. Travelling briskly, the little convoy creates a cloud of dust on the dirt road, it then slows down a little further on, reaches a bumpy slope, and finally stops at the entrance to a narrow path. The man leaves his seat and gets the beasts out of the van, regirths his horse and gets into the saddle, followed by the mules attached one to the other by their tails, and makes his way up the narrow path bordered with cactus and chaparrals, in order to reach the meager pastures where cows need salt.

As in love with efficiency and profitability as his ancestors, the cowboy, the rancher of today, uses the car, the plane, the C.B. and sometimes the computer, which saves time, avoids trouble, and limits the need for personnel. However, like his forefathers, he always has to come to terms with the harshness of his environment and take care of his livestock. Things would be impossible for him without the horse. The times of the long drives have certainly gone but in order to manage the pastures and the water holes, often surveyed by airplane or helicopter, the herds must continually be moved and driven from one pasture to another, from the mesa to a grassy canyon. And how could this be done in any other way than on horseback? Enclosures facilitate the annual roundup, but in the coming season only horsemen can reassemble the cows and calves and use the lasso to effect the branding which remains indispensable. These enclosures, which he detests since they are an encroachment on his liberty, can be watched on horseback and attended to should the occasion arise. Although enclosed, the wide open spaces constitute his universe, and the cowboy still watches over its dimensions, colours, and harshness. It is a fascinating world. Above all when seen from the height of a saddle, on which the cowboy lives, torn between the computer and legend of the West.

EFFICIENT HORSEMANSHIP (AND HORSES!)

The fact that the cowboy lives with one foot in the past has not meant, as far as we are aware, that he has lost his sense of efficiency. And whoever says efficiency says evolution, transformation and improvement. Also the man of the West today is very different from his forefathers in the harness that he uses, and the horsemanship that he practices, the horses he rides and the way in which he trains them. In every respect, he shows tolerance and imagination without worrying about accepted ideas or tradition.

The rider of the West is often a rodeo amateur. Consequently he has abandoned the saddle of Buffalo Bill's times, adapted to the necessities of his own era, and carries high a cantle and a raised pommel. The current roping saddle he uses is well equipped with a solid horn (pommel) to which the lasso can be fixed, but the seat is almost flat and his cantle is low so that he can mount rapidly. There are no rules as to the horse's bit and reins: the bridle and bit which suits the horse best is used. And the hackamore, is favoured by many. The multitude of types used here and there in order to achieve such and such a result, sadly cannot be described in these pages. An entire book would not be enough to do this!

The cowboy's horsemanship differs very little from that in Europe, but it corresponds perfectly to the requirements of his work and leisure. In general, but not always, for he takes no notice of any rules, he rides long trots seated (which can be done easily without the horse suffering) and guides his mount with his left hand, using the reins for support. As to this last point, this is nothing new! In order to keep one hand free to salute the ladies, Monsieur de La

movements are executed without the strict classicism of France.

The horses which the rider of the West mounts no longer have much in common with those which were at the disposal of his ancestors. And this is less because of their nature (breed or morphology) than because of their training. From where does the modern horse's quietness and obedience come? It is simply due to the manner in which it is trained, from the breaking of the horse, right up to the full dressage, previously done for economic reasons in the shortest possible time. The training of a young horse can now last months or even years. At the end of the twentieth century, everyone is in agreement that a docile and cooperative horse is not only agreeable for work, but also has a higher value. For the horse is nowadays most often bought by people who only envisage riding it during their leisure, who are neither horse-breakers nor trainers and who are consequently looking for a docile mount.

To describe in detail this training would be beyond the scope of this book, but let us demonstrate it by means a single example: the way in which a horse is made to walk at the sound of a voice. Held by hand, it first of all learns to walk and stop on command — a carrot or a tidbit is given as a reward for every successful execution of the command — and then to back up, turn to the left and lastly to the right, which is more awkward since whoever leads the horse generally leads it with the right hand. Thus one can arrive at the stage where the horse obeys every command without even being led by the reins. One could say that from the moment one comes to ride the horse, the rider has no trouble in making himself understood by means of the action of the reins. It is enough for him to accompany these actions with some brief and simple words which tell the horse which movement he expects of him.

There are a multitude of procedures of this type which make American horses so manageable. They are efficient horses.

The style of American horsemanship, inspired by those who work with animals, can seem brutal, but, done properly, it never hurts the horse.

Guérinière rode this way. If the Western equitation, efficient by necessity, is often the most instinctive, simple and useful, it can also be knowledgeable in the full sense of the word. And today it has masters like Monte Foreman in Colorado, who teaches his pupils how to gallop in less than five hours. At the end of a training course, performing a pirouette or trotting stiffly on the inner foot no longer seems to hold any secrets for his pupils, even if these

RIDERS FROM ALL WALKS OF LIFE

Are cowboys the only people to ride a horse in the United States? Of course not. In America, 70% to

80% of horsemen are in fact horsewomen. Just like men, they participate in all equestrian sports, from endurance tests to polo, horse racing, the so-called classic disciplines (show jumping, dressage and cross country) as well as the circuits. A great number of equestrian shows take place every weekend from Florida to Oregon, and from California to Kentucky. They may incorporate many feathered Indians (genuine or fake!) leading their horses by a cord passed around the lower jaw, gentlemen wearing huntsman's cap and gold-buttoned jacket, or cowboys straight from the great days: with coloured shirts, chaps and saddles of embossed leather. There is no class distinction here: everyone participates in the same spirit. Each one is a rider and nothing else.

HORSES BY THE MILLION

The list of all the types and breeds of horses which are ridden by all these riders for different purposes is a long one. Whatever the breed, a horse is judged above all else on the grounds of what type of work it is destined for, on its capacities and physical and psychological aptitudes. As for the beauty of the animal, that rarely constitutes a criterion in itself. It comes as a bonus and that is all.

All the same let us briefly examine a few typically American breeds. The quarter horse is the most popular horse in the United States. One figure proves this: that of the number of entries in the stud book: two million. This figure is the highest in the world. Selected originally to be entered in short-distance races (of a quarter mile, from whence its name comes), the quarter horse is a short horse with fine limbs. Its extremely developed hind-quarters allow for a flying start. Its feeling for livestock and its physical attributes make it the horse par excellence for ranch or rodeo.

The Morgan is above all enduring, economical and powerful. You recognize them immediately by their strongly-muscled necks and withers. All Morgans spring from a common ancestor: the legendary Justin Morgan. Docile and attentive in their work, they make excellent ranch and circuit horses.

Coloured horses, the Appaloosas and pintos, are many people's favorites, because their unique coat makes them a choice mount. They come in all sizes and shapes, since their colour is genetic rather than by transmission of characteristics specific to the breed.

We could also cite the Tennessee Walker, perfect on parade (and often used in the circus!), the American saddle horse, who walks the rack, the pony of the Americas, the small sized Appaloosa, or the American Shetland, who has Icelandic horses as its ancestors! Let's not forget the mustang, who still lives in the wild in deserts such as that of Nevada; and then the mule! It has its fans who organize annual races, even obstacle races!

The horse in North America has been part of daily life for a long time and will be for a long time to come.

Wild or not, the horse is always a symbol of liberty, above all in a country like America, where it made history.

In Argentina, as elsewhere, a horse used for work must be brought to the corral to be harnessed and saddled before setting out on a journey. It is the same for wild animals, from among which must be chosen the future mounts of gauchos, those caballero cowboys.

HORSES AND GAUCHOS

A brief look at the map of the South America shows that the areas propitious for horses and horse rearing are not widely spread in comparison to the size of the continent. Neither the peaks and the high plateaux of the Andes, nor Patagonia and the Land of Fire, and still less the immense Amazon forest, resemble the steppe, which is the preferable habitat for the horse. Yet, since its introduction into South America, the horse has not only adapted to the harshness of the Argentinean Pampas — a steppe 'blessed by the devil, — but it has also learnt how to adapt to environments which are very different, and thus give birth, here and there to unexpected breeds. And here, perhaps more than anywhere else in the world, it has influenced the existence of man, modeled his character, shaped his mentality and 'created' — the word may surprise, but is justified — a two-footed being, who like itself is the son of the wind and of liberty.

FROM ZERO TO INFINITY

The horse spread through South America much more quickly than it did north of Mexico: in one century as opposed to three. This rapid progression was essentially due to the horse breeders of the Caribbean Islands, which were the first territories conquered by the Spanish.

To begin with there was Pizarro who, in 1532, disembarked on the coast of Peru with about thirty horses. These did not have the same psychological impact on the Incas as those in the herds of Cortez had had in the same period on the Aztecs. However, as soon as the Inca empire was conquered, one of Pizarro's primary concerns was the establishment of stud farms. The conquistadors could not conceive of an army without cavalry.

The products of these stud farms were to contribute to the conquest of new territories and also, gradually, to provide almost the whole continent with horses.

Pedro de Vildavia, one of Pizarro's lieutenants, arrived in Chile in 1541, and in Patagonia in 1584. He ordered the setting up of stud farms in the oases of the desert and on the foothills of the Andes. Also, setting off from Peru, Diego de Rojas explored,

around 1542, what is today northern Argentina. In 1550, he was followed by Juan Nunez de Prado, who established a colony and a stud farm in the pleasant area of Tucuman. During various battles against Indian tribes, the Spanish lost dozens of stallions and mares, which, once free, multiplied almost to infinity.

Before examining them, let us travel to the Atlantic coast, and the site of Buenos Aires on the shore of the Rio de la Plata. It was around 1536 that Pedro de Mendoza, from Spain, disembarked with seventy horses. The colony, like the stud farm which was set up, was short-lived. Five years after their arrival, the Spanish found themselves besieged by the Indians. Very quickly they were reduced to eating their horses, with the exception, so they say, of five mares and seven stallions which they set free before hurriedly boarding their ships. About thirty years later, Juan de Garay re-established the colony on the Rio de la Plata, and was amazed to discover the pampas inhabited by innumerable herds of wild horses — or horses which had become wild. The first idea that occurred to him was that they were the descendants of the twelve horses which survived the siege of the city. It is much more probable — if not certain — that their ancestors were the dozens of horses which had fled from the region of Tucuman, down towards the south, where they were perhaps joined by the horses of Chile, and returned to the wild after having passed through the Cordilleras in the company of men. It seems improbable that only twelve horses would be able in thirty years to form a herd so numerous that it could, from afar evoke a forest. It is in the midst of these horses, and thanks to them, that those rough and free horsemen, the gauchos, emerged.

THE HORSE GIVES RISE TO A VERY SPECIAL HORSEMAN

The Pampas is a rough area, as flat as it is immense, and stretches from the Andes to the Atlantic and from Patagonia to the tropical zones. The winters there are polar, accompanied by a relentless wind, the pampero, and summers are so torrid that in

The importance of a mount in Brazil is shown in the form of these figurines representing riders on mules.

Buenos Aires, they say 'ten million inhabitants try to survive till the Autumn'.

It is a rugged horse that can survive such living conditions and manage to adapt to them. Ruthless natural selection has made it an economical animal, of sure foot and with a truly extraordinary endurance.

Equally, it is a rugged, strapping young man, the solitary gaucho, who responds to the challenging call of the Pampas, a land with a limitless sky, and who sets off for adventure and comes to terms with infinity, nothingness, and himself. To come to terms with a freedom which only the horse can provide. Thanks to the horse, distance is diminished, and dangers — flash floods, wild animals and the like — can be overcome so that food becomes easy to procure. Son and lover of the Pampas, the gaucho could not exist without the horse.

Who is this gaucho who appeared towards the end of the 16th century? A loner, he does not belong to any established group and refuses the constraints and the advantages of life in society. Neither does he belong to a precise ethnic group, and he may be white or an Indian half-breed, born on the continent or in Europe. A vagabond, obsessed with space and liberty, the only important thing for him is his eternal state of wandering. Nothing hinders his nomadic existence.

One horse or many? There are enough to capture (in the 17th century they were so numerous on the Pampas that anyone could take possession of all they wanted, up to a maximum of 10,000 head!).

Food? It is enough, at meal times, to lasso an ox, slaughter it and set aside the choicest cut. For just like the horse, the oxen brought by the first colonies very quickly multiplied to an enormous degree.

Money? In order to earn money, the gaucho sells his services to any cattle ranch. But he only resorts to work through necessity: most of the time he prefers dealing in the lucrative business of leather and skins, the primary wealth of the country. What does he do with the money, you may ask. He uses it to buy at the 'tavern' or 'bar', as well as at bistros and shops, 'teas', the ingredients of which compensate for the things lacking in his exclusively meat diet. He also uses it to gamble: gauchos are passionate about all games. Cock-fighting, cards and horseracing are for him an excuse to gamble away his last peso. And above all he does not tolerate a card sharp! As macho as he is violent, he will pull out his facon, a long knife, which he carries at the back of his large belt, and which can readily carve up a dishonest player, anyone who quarrels with him, or anyone who casts doubt upon his honour. Following such incidents he jumps into the saddle and disappears.

The prompt justice of this mad individualist, who ignores the law and for whom only his personal liberty and honour count, is evidently not to the taste of the authorities. From the end of the 18th century, the state has undertaken to bring into line the gaucho whose reputation as a smuggler and livestock thief has been solidly established for centuries. They have made vagabondage an offence and made it obligatory for every inhabitant of the Pampas to carry a work permit, regularly checked by employers, which the gaucho must present to any agent of public order. Under the threat of compul-

A livestock fair in Uruguay; the drivers, owners, sellers and buyers mingle in front of the enclosures. In the dust and the noise, the transactions commence. But it is also a chance for everyone to get out his most beautiful clothes and, for the peon to be proud of his future horse-riding son.

sory conscription into the army, the gaucho must submit to what he judges to be an eccentricity. His wandering is now limited. He can only change employer as often as is absolutely necessary. Yet gaucho he is and gaucho he remains.

HORSEMEN OF DANGER

His knowledge of the country and its fauna and his ability as a horseman, and even more his bravery and contempt for danger, make the gaucho a highly prized workhand by the estancieros (land owners). And most of the time, it is the more dangerous jobs, those refused by the permanent employees of the estancias, which the gaucho is given. Taking with him his tropilla (herd of a dozen horses), led by the madrina (a mare supplied with a bell), which allows him to change horses as often as necessary, he takes part in the gathering in of livestock and the movements of the herds. When the number of horses to break in is too big for the bronco-buster to carry out the task, it is he who is called in. When breaking in horses by force, he makes it a point of honour to choose the most difficult in order to show off his skills. In the northern territories, covered with rolling hills, cactus bush and thornbush which is difficult to penetrate, it is he who is charged with the dangerous hunt for deer or for pumas and mountain cats, which plague the herds and terrorize the population. He pursues the animal on horseback and captures it with his lasso or with las tres marias — the boleadoras, which are made up of three stones covered in leather and tied together by thin straps. Skillfully thrown, the boleadoras wrap round the back legs of the deer and paralyze it. It only remains for it to be killed. But not in any way! Neither with a rifle nor a hand gun, which the gaucho does not possess: but with a dagger! In the gaucho way!

Despite his courage and the relative stability which has been imposed upon him, the gaucho remains a contemptuous loner, a vagabond. How can you trust a man who makes some girl or other pregnant, as he pleases, at every port of call, and keeps his horse as his only family? How can you respect a man who so often makes his escape from the pursuit of the law only through the valor and endurance of his horse, after he has rendered his justice here or there? Yet this horseman, with neither hearth nor home, for whom institutions are only an infringement of his liberty, was to become, in little less than half a century, the soul of his country.

. . . AND DANGEROUS HORSEMEN

In 1808 South America rose in rebellion. Everywhere people stood up against the Spanish overseer. In Argentina, San Martin, the Liberator, called for gauchos to gather and take up arms against troops faithful to the Spanish crown. There is no doubt that political independence was of little importance to these men, who after all had only their horses and their liberty! But to fight on horseback was for them something more exciting than gathering in the cattle or indulging in smuggling! And they fought with an enthusiasm and a boldness which won the admiration even of their enemies. Wild hordes, they charged the regular troops, making use of, due to the lack of any other arms, their lassos, boleadoras and facones. Their ability in the saddle, their rapid maneuvers and their bravery when faced with formidable opponents, made them victorious. The gauchos, having defeated the royal troops, developed a taste for combat and for the pleasure of fighting on horseback, and participated in all the internal struggles which ravaged the country for so long. In the roughest of battles, it was not unusual for two parties of gauchos to find themselves on opposite sides!

This drawing of 1840 shows that the Indians were very used to the horse, as a pack animal but also as a mount, contrary to the llama, even though it was long domesticated.

What strange animals. Often the horses of cavalry which travelled near the Andes were frightened by the approach of the first llamas they had seen. The latter, on the other hand, remained unperturbed. After all, were they not at home?

Towards the end of the century, the fighting ceased. And it was then that the layabout, become warrior became a legend.

THE DREAM OF A POPULAR HERO

In spite of lacking certain qualities, real or imagined, the figure of the gaucho, the free horseman who fought for the independence of his country, is so fascinating and mysterious, poetic and powerful, that a number of great writers have made him the hero of many of their works. One of these, *Marin*

Fierro, an epic in verse by the poet José Hernandez, celebrates the gaucho with such power and simplicity that it immediately obtained an immense popular success. In it he affirms: 'My glory is to remain free as a bird in the sky'. The gaucho is no longer a layabout of the high road, but a national hero. A hero without a face with whom all Argentineans identify even to this day. A joyous horseman, who, galloping on his horse, carries the dreams of limitless space and liberty of an entire people.

A DIFFERENT SOMBRERO BUT THE SAME HORSE

As in times gone by, the gaucho of the 1980's wears a large belt which he loves to incrust with silver and pieces of money and in the back of which he carries his dagger with its carved handle. If he is always dressed in the traditional bombachas (baggy trousers), he has generally forsaken the pony-skin boots, cherished by his predecessors, for those of patent leather with pleats; and his sombrero and his poncho are now the shape and colour of his place of origin, since in modern times he is no longer a nomad, but belongs to a given place. Likewise Argentina is also gradually being invaded by the modern inventions which have overthrown the gaucho.

First it was refrigeration that gave meat a commercial value by permitting its conservation, and which at the same time prevented the gaucho from killing a fresh ox for each meal. Then came the railway, which allowed rapid transportation of the herds to the abattoir, thus eliminating for the most part the work of the horseman. Finally, barbed-wire fences criss-crossed the country and put a limit on the endless rides towards the horizon and the gauchos' magical liberty.

The gaucho of today hardly retains any of the habits and customs of his forefathers except his name and his horse. But what a horse!

FROM CONTEMPT TO FAME

For a long while, in order to obtain their horses, the Argentineans were content to take from the immense free herds. But at the end of the last century and the beginning of this one, they looked closely at importing European horses and raising them, forgetting the horse of the Pampas and even despising it, notably because of its modest size. The credit for having rediscovered the Criollo, the Creole horse, born in the wilderness of the Pampas, goes to Pro-

The attitude of the horseman at work is practically the same at all latitudes. Note the horseman with reins in one hand, the other hand free to hold any necessary tools — here a long pole. And also note the wide-brimmed flat hat which the Spanish caballeros call the sombrero, and not the callot, as the Mexicans do. As for the sheepskin on the saddle, it is typical of a country which mainly raises sheep. The halter adjusted underneath the horse's mouth is also common among working horsemen, as it is with riders who spend a long time in the saddle elsewhere. They all need to be able to tie up their horse as necessary.

170

fessor Emilio Solanet. Having gathered a number of this breed which showed the best of its qualities, he strictly controlled their reproduction and valued the offspring which extended the power, economical value, endurance, intelligence and longevity of his Criollos. Very quickly a fierce controversy divided advocates and disparagers of the horse from the Pampas. Professor Solanet put an end to this argument in a very curious way: by offering two of his horses to a schoolmaster who had decided to try to travel, by horse, from Buenos Aires to New York, no less! The idea seemed insane. To cover such a distance, strewn with so many obstacles, by horse, was truly a long shot.

One fine day in 1928, two and a half years after their departure from Buenos Aires, Mancha, Gato and their rider Aimé Félix Tschiffely, trotted onto Broadway. They had arrived at the end of a journey of 15,000 kilometers, which had been marked by a multitude of tests and had crossed some of the most inhospitable regions of the globe. The two Criollos

The training of young horses is not always an easy job especially for horse breeders who may not yet have selected which of their many animals will be the most docile in the future. Breaking is usually extremely quick and is a test of the will of the animal which must submit or else. It is only 'broken in' once, after which it will learn the rudiments of being ridden, and only then will it be chosen by a rider. The pursuit of its education by its new master will be gentle from then on In effect most of the time it will become attached to its master by good treatment and care relevant to the work demanded.

had proved the fantastic aptitudes of their breed: going from sea level, where they had always lived, to altitudes of 5,000 meters, surviving mountains and deserts of extreme temperatures, and feeding on whatever came their way, from sugar cane to the waterweed of Lake Titicaca, palm leaves, (and even tobacco leaves); covering stages remarkable as much for their length as for the difficulties they presented; moving across the most difficult and most rugged terrain, circumventing sand drifts and seeking out water from a long way off.

The names Mancha and Gato, as well as that of

172

the rider who had known so well how to lead them and take care of them, Aimé Félix Tschiffely, are known to all Argentineans. They belong to legend.

A MORE THAN RIGOROUS SELECTION

It would be wrong to say that after the successful tour of the famous trio, there was never any more doubt as to the exceptional qualities of the Criollos. Though there were many who, in the manner of Professor Solanet, set about rearing horses from the semi-wild state. The Association of Breeders of Creole horses was formed, of which the aim was not only the maintenance of the qualities of the breed, but also their development. If that was possible! The breeding stock were carefully chosen by morphological criteria (size 1.38m to 1.50m, the colour of coat was unimportant — more than a hundred shades and sub-shades were registered —, bushy horse hair, an ample chest, muscled hindquarters and large back, lean limbs and short shanks). But these criteria were not always adhered to and every type and behaviour were tested by an assortment of tests of speed and manageability. As for endurance,

All working horsemen in the world have their games, which show off their acquired skills at festivals. And during their normal work, you can rely on them to do their best.

it was tested in competitions. The most famous, the marcha consisted of making the horse cover 750 kilometers in fourteen days, carrying a minimum of 110 kilos — harness and rider — and feeding it exclusively throughout the whole ordeal as well as as the preceding week on nothing more than grass! Surprising? It is still more so when you consider that the animal that has finished this test, without having been stopped by the judges or the vets is, on arrival, slightly thinner but as just as strong as on the day of departure. One detail to note: Only the horses are noted and classed. Not the riders.

Those who are familiar with the qualities of the Criollo, its engaging and willing character, and a bewildering aptitude for survival, can only be surprised to learn the extent to which it is neglected in the rest of the world. An explanation? Argentinean nonchalance perhaps. . .

THE FESTIVAL OF THE CRIOLLO

One of the favourite words of the Argentineans is: mañana (tomorrow). But there are occasions when they know how to rouse themselves quickly and efficiently, and these are when, in Buenos Aires or in a remote village in the provinces, there comes the

The difference between the Renaissance horseman of the church of Saint-Dominique at Salvador de Bahia and the keeper of livestock is great. And yet one gave the other, as with the stitched saddle, inspiration for the working saddle.

In the Amazonian marsh lands like the Mato-Grosso, exist herds. And for guarding buffalos and oxen nothing is better than a horse: water, mud, dusty roads, grass or gravel, nothing prevents it doing its work.

time to celebrate the Criollo. Everyone takes the festival's success very seriously. Early in the morning trucks bring, often over large distances, horses which will take part in the competitions and shows. All have been groomed with great care, have had their manes shaven, and the hairs in their ears and even their noses trimmed. Their gauchos, in keeping with tradition, make a great fuss over the harness. And the habilments of the horse are often no less rich than those of the rider. The bridle, lined in silver, sometimes weighs more than ten kilos! Stirrup irons, bars and leathers are also often decorated with heavy silver and it is not unusual for the visible part of the saddle-bow of the recado (the gaucho saddle) also to be encrusted with the same metal.

Throughout the day there are successive displays of the horses, by hand and mounted. And, very often, the judges are seconded by a jury. . . of children! Youngsters judge the animals which file past, covet-

ing the prize which will go to the youngster whose judgment is nearest to that arrived at by the adults. This is fine training for future horsemen, is it not?

Then come the tests of speed and manageability, which generally consist of slaloms between barrels. Next is the doma, a show of wild horses rather similar to that which takes place in the United States; exercises using the long leather lasso, on foot and on horseback, and other equestrian games which are followed with passion by a public as fanatical as it is knowledgeable. Whoever succeeds in remaining mounted does honour to the asado, the pieces of meat which since morning have been grilling on spits planted in the soil around a wood fire. The

176

asador (the official cook) carves juicy tidbits and suggests that they be washed down with the traditional mate as well as, a sign of the times, some Coca-Cola! Evening comes, and the bearded gauchos take up guitars and accordions. They have a great time dancing and playing the tango, of course, but they also celebrate in verse or prose the immense Pampas and the intelligent toughness of the Criollo.

NOVICE HORSEMEN

Other than the Criollo and the racing thoroughbred, two types of horse are mainly found in Argentina: the polo pony and the mestizo.

Raised in the rich ranches of the province of Buenos Aires, on the rich pastures of the humid Pampas, the polo pony does not belong to a particular breed. In order to obtain a fast, manageable and enduring animal, different horses of all origins are crossed without discrimination. And the Argentinean polo pony often has Criollo blood in him. His reputation is established: he is prized by polo players all over the world.

As his name suggests, the mestizo is also a crossbreed, a bastard, which may be beautiful or may take the appearance of an old crock. This is the common horse that is allowed to reproduce without selection and, mounted or harnessed, circulates throughout the Pampas. For the people of the campo, the countryside, he is an indispensable auxiliary. And perhaps this is less because of a lack of motor vehicles than because of the nature of the terrain. As soon as it rains on the Pampas, the dirt roads turn into slippery mud-baths on which car tires can only skid. Also, to take, for example, his milk churns to the village, the farmer harnesses his mestizo to a light cart whose high wooden wheels he has replaced with pneumatic wheels, similar to those of a car, and which skid like them. For this same reason, the novice arrives on horseback at his classes, holding his satchel in front of him. The approaches to the school often have the look of those of a Western saloon! It is not unusual to see a dozen or more horses, attached to the rail and waiting calmly for their young masters to finish their exercises.

THE HORSES OF A CONTINENT

If you were to embark on a tour of the equine livestock South America, in Brazil, Chile, Peru and Colombia among others places, you would find Criollos. But they would be Creole horses of a slightly different type and makeup than those of their near Argentinean cousins, having been changed by the living conditions experienced in their areas of origin. All, however, are of Argentinean blood, for breeders, whether Brazilian or Uruguayan, have appreciated for a long time the quality of the horses of the Pampas and have imported them more or less regularly. The ties between the breeders of Criollos in all the Latin American countries are so close that they have formed an international association for economic reasons, but also for the pleasure of being united in their interest in the same subject.

Despite the small number of places suitable for horse-rearing in South America, particular and sometimes original species have been developed here and there: in Brazil, the Mangalargo, a trotter with long limbs and pronounced withers, and the Campolino, a semi-draught horse; in Chile, the Chilean Caballo, somewhat similar to the North American quarter horse. And in Peru there are some real phenomena. First, of all let us cite the Morucha and the Chimbivileno, ponies who live in the Andes at altitudes which are often higher than 4,000 metres. And then let us move on to the famous Peruvian Caballo de Paso.

The Peruvian Paso is a spectacle! First, it surprises with its panache and its bushy hair, which gives it the air of an Andalusian horse. Then it surprises still more with the disproportion between its forequarters and hindquarters, the former with its excessively striking breast and enormous girth, appearing hyperdeveloped when compared to the latter. Finally, it surprises as soon as it starts moving, by moving its front legs in the same way as a swimmer doing the crawl. It moves with the paso llano, a type of amble, and can, at a more or less rapid pace, keep up this gait over considerable distances. The paso llano is extremely comfortable for the rider. Judge for yourself: In order to prove the total absence of jolts in its step, the Peruvians put a glass of water full to the brim on the saddle. They start the horse

off and make it cover a hundred, five hundred, or even more metres. when they stop him not a single drop of water has been spilt. A draught and work horse in the sugar cane plantations of the Peruvian coast, the area where it is bred, the Paso, in his carriage, as unique as it is brilliant, is still a magnificent parade horse. And this is why the entire world comes to buy it and regards it as one of the most beautiful of horses, and why it is one of the prides of Peru.

THE UNIVERSAL HORSE

The thoroughbred racehorse is of course raised in the Americas: in the United States or in Argentina, and is found everywhere, from Canada to Argentina, on a multitude of race tracks. The Argentinean, racetracks are full at every meeting. Those in North America are sometimes the size of a small town. And in order to satisfy the tourist's passion for the sport in Panama — where the climate makes horse breeding almost impossible — planeloads of champions are brought in from Tennessee, Argentina and even Europe.

It is not so much moving the cattle which is difficult, it is steering them The herd is a fused mass which goes according to the direction taken by its most advanced point and which possesses a momentum of its own, which can crush the animals in front if they come to an abrupt halt. Therefore everything is affected by changing the direction of the head of the herd, sometimes involuntary when animals sense water or fresh grass, despite the fences.

A European trainer travelling round the race tracks of the New World could not fail to be amazed. In Colorado or Florida, he would discover electric leading reins used in order to lead the horses around a precise track; he would be surprised to see, in the early morning, the stable lads warming up the thoroughbreds harnessed with the saddles of cowboys! On the shores of the Rio de la Plata, he would be perplexed by the presence at training tracks of Criollos, none of them sized for racing, but which the gauchos mount in order to communicate their calmness to the nervous thoroughbreds.

But he would find horses similar to those which he is used to coming into contact with. Horses which, even though born in the heart of the humid Pampas or in the bluegrass of the State of Kentucky, are really just superb machines for speed and not the true American horse.

179

THE ISLANDS

On the Equator between the Indian and Pacific oceans, Asia is no longer a continent, but a multitude of islands. The Indonesian archipelago is both mountainous and swampy; between the great volcanic chains are river valleys covered with luxuriant vegetation and oppressed with a hostile climate. It is therefore on the high plateaux, cultivated with rice, that civilization has developed. The social geography has been overturned by the recent demographic explosion in these regions. The horse has never been very much at ease in equatorial climates and even in the more northerly Philippines, its breeding has never really flourished. The uncomfortable land surfaces of these territories do not suit an animal such as the horse. Besides, local tradition attributes the introduction of the horse (as well as that of all domestic animals) in the islands, to the arrival of ancestors by canoe! And if you can accept that a number of species could have preceded man on these few rather remote lands of the Asiatic continent, it is very probable that the horse did not multiply in the wild in these regions which are so inhospitable for him. Besides the traditional customs relating to horses are too near certain rites of the Indian peninsula not to suggest a concomitant migration of these peoples and their mounts.

However, the Philippines, a long time Spanish colony, whose population is in the majority Christian, no longer presents other than rare traces of its ancient history. There the horse is only a work companion, a pack animal or draught horse which the precarious economy of that region cannot replace by motor vehicles. Only the bloody (but very popular) custom of stallion fighting persists: two young

In the Sunda Islands, the welcoming ceremony takes place on horseback, like here, in the village of Seba (Island of Sabu).

181

male horses, ungelded, are released into a ring in the presence of a mare. As the bets multiply, the bidding progresses and the combat between the two suitors becomes more savage. For the most part a game of chance, this custom persists, and neither the Spanish (great lovers of horses) before their departure and the independence of these islands, nor succeeding governments, have been able (or have wanted to?) prevent it.

DANCES AND BATTLES IN THE SUN

Indonesia itself is more rich in equestrian tradition. This is the result of the very strong Arab influence. The Arab traders explored these parts long before the Westerners, and the Muslim religion still largely predominates in this equatorial archipelago. It is also suggested that the later Dutch commercial imprint on the Sunda Islands, since making its first appearance nearly two centuries after the arrival of the Spanish in the Philippines, influenced the indigenous civilization? Either way the horse keeps an important place in the social and religious life of the Indonesians.

Thus the horse remains, as in the past, tied to all the symbolic stages of life: birth, marriage, and death, as well as seed sowing and religious festivals. Of course, it is no longer buried with the Rajah, for whom it was the sign of wealth and power. Since the 14th century, and without doubt as a result of the Arab influence, horse breeding developed remarkably in certain islands, and the sovereigns of Sumba and Sumbawa in particular (the two biggest islands) made a fortune through the production and export of horses. Beyond even this economic importance, the rite of the horse accompanying his master into the kingdom of the dead was of preeminent importance. And now that the era of the Rajahs is past, the role of the horse remains just as important for the general population. The cult of ancestors continued and the horse remained for the Indonesians the best messenger to influence those powers which were necessary to ensure successful harvests and commerce. Thus there were still sacrifices of horses, slaughtered for important funerals!

Less cruel are the traditional jousts, mimicking the numerous battles and skirmishes of past centuries, for the possession of the herds. The lances are no longer iron but are of wood. The worth accorded to the victor (or scorn to the defeated) and the prestige (or the humiliation) for the clan concerned are so important, that the game often degenerates, and frequently turns into a drama: a fallen rider will always want to redeem himself even if he has been trounced by his adversary!

Still more significant is the persistence of the very ancient rite, the dance of the horse (Kuda lumping), less dangerous than the aforementioned pasola (joust). It is a ceremony in which the participants, under the influence of a Dukum (a ritual figure, half doctor, half priest) dance and throw themselves about until they go into a trance, the convulsions of which are felt to represent the purification and exorcism of evil powers. Like horse sacrifices, these dances are less and less common, although recent reports indicate the total participation of Sumba ponies in this ritual, dancing with their hooves and neighing to the rhythm of the music. But it seems nowadays that the animal is often replaced by hand-painted wooden effigies decorated with a carefully plaited raffia mane.

THE LITTLE HORSE
AND ITS FINERY

The protagonist, even if it has many different names (most often that of its island), is practically identical from island to island; whether it be on Bali, Java, Timor, Sumba or Sumbawa, the Indonesian pony is small — 1.20 m to 1.25 m — and rather slender, with a rather primitive look about him. Only the Batak, raised and selected in the stud farms of Sumatra, presents a more distinguished silhouette, as well as greater height and more agreeable looks, closer to that of his Arab ancestors, imported by merchants in the 14th century. But as is always the case in a difficult climate for horses, the variations can be important as far as what sort of work it does and how it is cared for (above all its food).

The important value (as much economic as religious) possessed by the horse protects it from ex-

Indonesian ponies are small with a dark coat; and for decoration their manes are plaited with grasses. Some of them even have their legs armed with points of bamboo. They are ridden bareback with a light rope harness in which no metal is to be found. Their riders do not maintain any particular equestrian tradition and keep their ceremonial habits in order to mount their small horse.

tinction, an exception being made of course for the rare sacrifices still practiced. Outside of work, when they are most often ridden bareback and without a bridle bit, the sacred ceremonies see them adorned with harnessing of coconut fibre, with multi-coloured ribbons and pieces of silver or ivory. And the way of life of a clan or a village keeps time with these equestrian rituals, although the notion of the horse messenger between this world and the next is hardly compatible with the current religion of Islam! But this only seems to be a paradox, since, along with a new faith, the Arabs brought to the Indonesian archipelago horses of high quality, which were able to improve the local livestock and to allow at the same time the creation of a source of new local wealth, horse breeding, and an ideal support to a popular belief too deep to disappear under the torrent of influences from foreigners and the modern world. Perhaps the Indonesian pony is the last remaining sacred horse.

HORSEMEN OF A NEW WORLD

'Terra australis incognita' is how unimaginative cartographers described the Australian continent from 1550 onwards, and it remained unknown for centuries. Dutch navigators explored its rivers in all directions and baptized it New Holland, but they hardly ventured inland at all. It was only in 1788, after England had officially taken possession, that the first fleet dropped anchor in what was to become Sydney and the first colonists, seven hundred convicts and rebels, taken from the prisons of his Gracious Majesty, disembarked.

The exiles discovered that this continent really was a New World, with inhabitants, fauna and flora totally different from that which they were used to. They were baffled by the primitive aborigines and their society, which they found difficult to understand; they were unprepared for the sight of the eucalyptus tree with its heady perfume, the tree fern and so many other trees and plants with delicate and dazzling flowers; and they were surprised by koala bears, emus, kangaroos and the collared lizard. This country, disconcerting because of its climate, variation and almost endless countryside, offered the Europeans few means of subsistence. So, grain, plants and animals, including oxen and cattle, were very quickly imported, as were, of course, horses.

The Australian bronco ride is directly inspired by the American rodeo: the same costume, the same rules and the same strap tied at the groin of the wild horse to make it buck.

GOLD FITTINGS!

No one really knows what type of horse first arrived in this country of dingoes and marsupials. But it is probable, that they came from England, and according to experts, many might have come from the Welsh mountains.

How they reached this continent, situated on the other side of the world, is a question with no answer. The only certainty is that about fifty years after the arrival of the first horses, they were sufficiently numerous to be exported and it was from Australia that New Caledonia, in 1851, imported their first horses.

According to the evidence, the first Australians imported some horses from Europe, and bred them for use with the saddle and harness. Then in 1793 pioneers arrived who were not convicts, but free men, hungry for land and profit. Animals participated in the colonization of this gigantic country and horses of stockmen, or breeders, were used to drive the enormous herds of cattle and sheep. But the process was less rapid than you might suppose. For many of the settlers were novices in the subject of breeding and could not accept the fact that livestock could constantly live in the open and roam free. In the Old Continent, thousands of beasts were returned to the stables every evening, by herdsmen on foot.

The mid 19th century also marked the beginning of the Gold Rush. Certain reefs turned out to be so rich in precious metals that miners, having made a fortune within a few days, paid homage to their horses in iron, or gold!

BRUMBIES, DONKEYS AND DROMEDARIES

From the start of colonization, explorers, breeders, and miners, as well as convicts and bandits, lost or abandoned wounded or unneeded horses in the bush.

Now wild, the descendants of these animals, the brumbies, roamed across the immense savannas of the northern and central territories, where civilization did not disturb their peace. In later years, a number of contagious diseases, and persecution from farmers who accused these horses of ravaging their fields led to lessening their numbers.

The horses that survived lived in small herds, very often without an area of their own, roaming around in search of food, which was as scarce as rainfall. Many people consider these horses worthless because of excessive in-breeding, but others are sure that the ruggedness of the country and climate give them a surprising hardiness and a positive survival instinct. In order to ascertain who is correct, it might be necessary to imitate certain stockmen, capture a few brumbies, break them in, ride them and then judge.

One interesting detail is that while in the bush the brumbies came into close contact with herds of donkeys who had also been returned to the wild, and also dromedaries! The latter had been imported from Afghanistan — with their camel-drivers — in order to resolve the problems of transport in the semi-desert areas. Set free after the arrival of the train and the motor vehicle, they are today the only wild camels living in the world.

Ah! yes: what does the word brumby mean? It seems that this name is a derivative of burambie, which in Aborigine means flying freely. From that we might deduce that Pegasus is of Australian origin!

HELICOPTER, MOTORBIKE AND HORSE

Before travelling further across the Australia of yesterday and today, let us glance over the smallest continent, which is also the largest island in the world. Its surface area is about fourteen times that of France, but there are only 16 million

Stockmen have much to do in the Australian savannah in order to contain, with a few riders, the enormous herds which they round up for branding or regular vaccination.

inhabitants. Moreover, more than half the population live in the capitals of seven states, so the greater part of the country is almost deserted. In the limitless open spaces, the most common human activity is raising merino sheep and cattle. Cattle number nearly 30 million head, and you can count some 130 million sheep. In order to look after them and move these enormous herds, it is of course necessary to use horsemen. However, the number used is much less than one might imagine.

Nowadays, the stockmen whom you meet on the bush trails are more likely to be riding a powerful motorcycle than a frisky steed. The jeep, the light aircraft and the helicopter — which is piloted with remarkable courage and skill — also allow them to guide, regroup and drive the beasts towards water holes or new pasture. Stockmen still wear big felt hats, jeans, and traditional boots, but, concerned with being as efficient as possible, they have abandoned the horse for more high-performance machines, which often means that just three or four men can properly tend to herds of ten or fifteen thousand head.

The previous vast domains, where sometimes

more than two hundred hectares barely fed one cow, have been split up and their pastures improved, by irrigation and the planting of nitrogen-fixing plants, so that nowadays barely five hectares is needed per head. This is what has made the job of breeding livestock so easy. But it has taken away the important role which the horse possessed not so long ago. The horse is still far from being a thing of the past. Better still, it stands a chance of regaining a certain importance in the economic plan of the future. Bizarre? Let's see!

DROUGHT AND GRAZING LAND

In order to understand something of the role of the horse and rider in the life of the stations, the Australian version of American ranches, let us take a look at one in more detail. Viewed from the sky, it often looks curious. Tracks and roads are outlined in and around its buildings, which are situated on the vast and deserted bush land, an intertwining of plant life which is as clear as it is fantastic. Not far from the barns, a landing area for helicopters lies near the corral where horses wait to be saddled. Round about there is endless space, colorful, engaging, and dominated by the high windmills used for pumping water. The number of hectares for one station can vary between several thousand to a few million according to the rainfall of the place, and the possibilities for irrigating and improving the grazing land. What is raised here? Sometimes sheep, the famous merinos with their surprising capacity to adapt; sometimes cattle, of one sort or another, depending on the climate and the quality of pasture. The sheep are still numerous, despite the competition facing wool since the end of the last war, from synthetic fabrics. As for cattle, the growing world market for meat has increased their numbers. In the temperate areas, Herefords are generally kept, whilst in hotter climates, Asiatic species, such as Brahmans are preferred. Attempts at cross-breeding to obtain animals which adapt to such and such a condition or country, have been and still are very frequent.

Life at the station is of course determined not only by the rhythm of the needs of the livestock, but also by periods of drought, which are sometimes disastrous. With regard to this last point, let us recall the mass slaughter which was caused by the drought of 1944, in which twenty thousand head of cattle perished. In difficult times like these, the stockman is dependent on the horse for survival. For it is in the saddle, and only in the saddle, that he can guide his beasts — above all the sheep — over the long pastures. During the weeks and months, he drives his herd along the roads, along the sides of which, thanks to damp ditches, grass of a more or less green colour, still grows. This movement of the herds from dried-out pasture lasts until the rain allows fodder to grow again on the lands of the station.

There are many other cases where the horse is, and will always be, indispensable to the stockman: for driving livestock, for gathering them in from particularly uneven ground, and also for the simple pleasure of riding across the wide open spaces.

THE STOCK HORSE

What type of horse does this stockman, or ringer, as the Australian cowboy is sometimes called, possess? Although it is to be found everywhere, it is always called by the same name and does not belong to a definite breed. This is for two reasons. First of all, the fact that Australia is made up of deserts, mountains, prairies, semi-arid and very arid areas, meant that it did not develop in one particular place and or into a particular breed. Next, horse breeders, forever worried, about efficiency, have their own exact ideas on how the work horse should be and, in order to improve their stock in one area or another, they do not hesitate to cross-breed them with thoroughbreds or quarter horses. So what is demanded of the stock horse? It must be intelligent (above all have a feeling for livestock), docile, manageable and enduring — despite the utilization of the motorcycle and aircraft, whole days spent in the saddle are frequently the stockman's lot. And it is because of these necessities that every breeder, without prejudice against any breed, selects and cross-breeds various types of horse. So it is difficult to describe the stock horse, which when all is said and done

does not really exist as a breed itself and even less so morphologically.

The breed which is not a breed in the proper sense, has one precise characteristic: its aptitude for work, since it is primarily that on which the selection is based. Throughout the many horse shows, of which the most prestigious is the Royal Melbourne Show, less emphasis is placed on the competitions of models and behaviour, than on the comparison of animals confronted with tests which recreate working conditions with livestock. The best way to make our own judgment on this type is again to go to Australia and ride a few stock horses!

In the first three or four years of his life, the foal

As in all countries where the horse has been introduced late, the initial inhabitants have very quickly adapted to the new way of life that it represents. Often, even the people close to nature have shown a very pronounced equestrian talent. In Australia, whether it be an aborigine or a half-caste, a good horseman is always in demand for the treks.

lives in total freedom, and is only touched once by man: during the indispensable operation of branding. After it is captured, broken in and trained for work, its owner's skill in cross-breeding horses is assessed. A successful cross-breed can make its owner the toast of Australian Stock Horse Society, which brings together some 13,000 breeders, and a stud book which has more than 30,000 entries.

These figures show the importance of a good cow horse in Australia. An importance which perhaps will continue to grow because of the treks, and convoying livestock over long distances.

If the silhouettes in the semi-light bring confusion about the country where this scene takes place, the vegetation in the middle of which the drivers regroup their herd is typical of Australia. It is between the thorny bushes and under the eucalyptus that the stockmen often work, in the dust and outside the hours of full sun.

THE OVERLANDERS

To raise cows and calves in remote regions, with vast free spaces, is one thing. To sell a herd, grazing hundreds of miles from the nearest city, port and market, is another and is of utmost importance. To bring the livestock to the consumer or the exporter is a big problem, one which was posed at the beginning of colonization. The crux of it is making the herd walk to the sailing departure point, across lonely country and deserts without water. It seems the first to tackle this type of work was a young Englishman, Joseph Hawdon, who in 1836, aided by a few friends, succeeded in driving a herd, which arrived in a very good state, more than four hundred

189

American and Australian entertainments of the rodeo are identical; this is not surprising, their riders do the same work.

miles to Port Philip. Since this first, riders who have been named the overlanders have up until recently continued to convoy herds across the whole continent, in every direction, towards all ports and along a multitude of rough and not so rough trails.

The reputation of some of these trails still lives on; that of the Birdsville Track, for example, dotted with carcasses of animals that died of thirst, has not been used for a long time.

In 1868, the overlanders became so numerous that the herds they guided posed problems to the breeders whose lands they crossed. A law was made to restrict their tramping over land and their right of access to the wells and pools. A permit to move herds was even introduced, but over the last ten years, diesel motors capable of pulling veritable trains on the road have rendered this permit obsolete.

So, is this the end of the treks? Certainly not. The current low price of meat, which is going to rise, coupled with an increase in the cost of automobile transport, makes, according to many, a return to the old method of convoying by horse riders look very profitable; and this would give the stock horse back an importance which is partly lost.

IN THE SADDLE!

The dawn sweeps the pastel-coloured sky. In the relative freshness of the morning, Peter rubs down a small grey horse. Today, it eats hay from mechanized engines! As a half-caste, he is avid for freedom and wandering, as were his aboriginal ancestors, and is happy to spend a day in the saddle, searching for the stray livestock which the helicopter spotted yesterday. The horse has been combed and fed and watered, and now Peter puts on the saddle cloth, and then the saddle itself. This Australian saddle is unique in its conception, without a pommel horn but with perfect balance, and with the raised cantle, it is deep and comfortable with its thigh and knee padding arranged on the very long, wide quarters. Peter bridles his horse and climbs into the saddle, holding his long whip of kangaroo skin.

The day advances. The sun burns. Keeping his hat over his eyes, Peter, with a click of the tongue, starts his horse off in a small gallop. From a flock of birds in the sky, he guesses that there is a water hole nearby, beside which he thinks he may find a few cows. There's the hole. He trots again. Peter cracks his whip to scatter the birds which almost attack him. The grey horse drinks. There is not a cow in sight.

On foot, to allow his mount to drink, Peter drifts away from the watering place. Gradually he loses himself, and becomes entranced by the breadth of the immense Australian land — sprinkled with coloured rocks, dotted with scanty greenish trees — and its vast panorama of liberty.

ACKNOWLEDGMENTS

This book was only made possible thanks to the collaboration of lovers of the horse and those fascinated by art and archeology. Jean-Louis Nou and Bertrand de Perthuis would like to express their appreciation to the following:

Maharani Gayatri Devi, His Excellency the Maharajah Bhawani Singh, of the Royal House of Jaipur; His Excellency Maharaj Arvind Kumar, of the Royal House of Udaipur;

The Prince of Wankaner, Thakur Sangaram Singh and Sani of Mandawa;

His Excellency the Maharajah of Mysore;

The Department of Indian Tourism in New Delhi and Paris;

Princess Alia, of the Hashemite royal family of Jordan;

His Excellency Prince Ali and Princess Wijdan;

Santiago and Ursula Lopez; Dr. Marchis and Pierre Simon, in Amman;

Mr. Michel Hamarneh of the Jordanian Tourist Board and Mr. Nagri Attalah;

Sheikh Solyman Abu Fawzi of Azrak;

The Ambassador of France; J.-Alain de Sedouy; Mr. Fawzy Zayadine;

The Spanish National Tourist Board in Paris and Mr. Rodas;

The Hungarian National Office of Tourism in Paris and Budapest; Mr. Harbulla;

The National Board of Stud Farms in Morocco;

The F.R.A.M. Society, Mr. Raimbault, and the P.L.M. company for their collaboration on the Moroccan trip;

Transtours and Madame Hélène Rabate, who opened the doors of Mongolia for them; Alia, with Mr. Frémy and Mrs. Duvernois.

The travel companies Sita World Travel in Paris and New Delhi, Business Travel Service in New Delhi and Kuoni France;

Photographic collaboration: Agfa-Gevaert for the Agfachrome films with which the photographs were taken;

Mamiya-France for its photographic equipment, as well as Godard- Flashomatic for its electronic lights;

Arka Laboratory and Madame Gorne for their developing work;

Miss C Levy; Mrs. Garot; Mr. Simonneau; Mr. Van Stratten; Mr. Delru; Michel Gaillard; Mr. Chehu, Director of Horse Magazine, Mr. Alhuwalia, Michel Buntz of the photographic agency Explorer;

Miss Jeanine Auboyer, Constance Rameaux, Jean-François Ballereau, all the Nathan team, Monique Nou, Philippe Ploquin, Professor Vadime, and Danielle Elisseeff, Michel Cartier, Miss Sugita, Mr Naqshband, Floréal Gavalda.

PHOTOGRAPHIC REFERENCES

The illustrations of this book are largely the work of JEAN-LOUIS NOU, who also carried out the iconographic research, working closely with the following agencies and photographers:

J-P ABADIE: pages 148, 156. ARENES-VINCENT PHOTOS: 116. BIBLIOTHEQUE NATIONALE, PARIS: 107, 146-147. F.CHEHU: 125, 134, 139, 140, 159. DIAF/Degroise: 143. EXPLORER: 22-23, 24, 27, 35, 36-37, 68, 105, 120, 121, 123, 124, 144, 145, 168; Baumgartner: 25; Desjardins: 72; Dubois: 176; Dupont: 113, 114-115; Errath: 165, 174; Ferrero: 184, 190; Gaubert: 30; Gérard: 179; Gohier: 162-163, 166-167, 171, 172, 175, 177, 180-181, 183; Hug: 73; Joffre: 99; Loirat: 67; Perno: 32, 39; Roy: 29; Thibaut: 93. GIRAUDON: 2, 136. A.PERIER: 186, 188, 189. C.POULET: 149, 152, 153, 154, 155, 157. C. RAMEAUX: 137, 141, 151, 160, 167, 169, 173. RAPHO/Michaud: 71, 92. J. VERTUT: 118, 119.